ROUTLEDGE LIBRARY EI
ECONOMICS AND SOC

Volume 17

THE INDUSTRIAL

THE INDUSTRIAL CRISIS

Its Causes and Its Lessons

K. E. EDGEWORTH

Routledge
Taylor & Francis Group
LONDON AND NEW YORK

First published in 1933 by George Allen & Unwin Ltd.

This edition first published in 2026
by Routledge
4 Park Square, Milton Park, Abingdon, Oxon OX14 4RN

and by Routledge
605 Third Avenue, New York, NY 10158

Routledge is an imprint of the Taylor & Francis Group, an informa business

British Library Cataloguing in Publication Data
A catalogue record for this book is available from the British Library

ISBN: 978-1-032-97576-4 (Set)
ISBN: 978-1-041-14093-1 (Volume 17) (hbk)
ISBN: 978-1-041-14094-8 (Volume 17) (pbk)
ISBN: 978-1-003-67294-4 (Volume 17) (ebk)

DOI: 10.4324/9781003672944

Publisher's Note
The publisher has gone to great lengths to ensure the quality of this reprint but points out that some imperfections in the original copies may be apparent.

Disclaimer
The publisher has made every effort to trace copyright holders and would welcome correspondence from those they have been unable to trace.

THE INDUSTRIAL CRISIS

ITS CAUSES AND ITS LESSONS

by

LIEUT.-COLONEL K. E. EDGEWORTH
D.S.O., M.C., A.M.I.E.E.

LONDON
GEORGE ALLEN & UNWIN LTD
MUSEUM STREET

FIRST PUBLISHED IN 1933

PRINTED IN GREAT BRITAIN BY
UNWIN BROTHERS LTD., WOKING

PREFACE

To Dr. George O'Brien, Professor of Economics in University College, Dublin, I tender my grateful thanks for the help and encouragement which he has given at every stage in the preparation of this essay.

K. E. E.

CONTENTS

THE INDUSTRIAL CRISIS

CHAPTER I

INTRODUCTION

THE SCOPE AND PURPOSE OF THE PRESENT ESSAY

WIDELY different reasons have been put forward to account for the financial and industrial crisis through which the world is now passing.

It has been suggested that the whole business is a bankers' ramp, that it is due to bankers' ignorance, or to defects in the currency system, or to war debts and reparations, or to tariffs and currency restrictions, or to over-production resulting from the excessive employment of automatic machinery, or to a number of other different causes.

The proposed remedies are even more varied. They include throwing the bankers into prison to make them disgorge their ill-gotten gains, reform of the currency system, bimetallism, cancellation of war debts and reparations, reduction or abolition of tariffs and currency restrictions, nationalisation of the banking system, nationalisation of industry, nationalisation of everything, and so on.

Some of the many amateur economists who have contributed to this flood of literature fall into definite errors, of which the commonest is the belief that an unlimited expansion of credit is a sure road to industrial prosperity. Reviewing the situation as a whole, however, the impression created on the mind of the present writer is that the majority of expositions lay undue emphasis on some particular factor or some particular aspect of the problem. In this manner a sense of proportion is lost and a distorted view is obtained of the problem as a whole.

Turning to the standard text-books on the other hand, the seeker after knowledge learns with some surprise that the orthodox theory of Economics is still in the making. Many well-known treatises contain a great deal of descriptive material which cannot be dismissed as irrelevant but which is certainly very imperfectly digested. They require for their perusal a critical judgement and a good deal of time.

The whole theory being still the subject of acute controversy, the professional economist naturally addresses his remarks mainly to his professional brethren and writes in consequence in technical language. In dealing with current events he is compelled to justify his opinions by entering into a wealth of detail which tends to conceal the main points at issue from the comprehension of the ordinary reader. For these reasons the writings of professional economists do not usually make easy reading.

It is impossible, however, to dismiss the theory of Economics as a matter in which ordinary men and women have no interest, and which is therefore properly left in the hands of specialists. Far from this being the case the individual citizen's actions, political and social, are of vital importance in determining the policy of governments and the general progress of events. It must further be remembered that political and economic mistakes have to be paid for, and that it is the individual citizen who ultimately pays for the blunders that have been made whether by himself or by others acting on his behalf. It is therefore the clear duty of business men and business women to study economic problems and to acquire an elementary knowledge of economic laws, a knowledge which they would certainly consider to be indispensable in relation to other problems of everyday life.

The present essay is intended to give a brief survey of the causes which have led up to the industrial crisis and to indicate the lessons which should be drawn from it. In writing it I have tried to keep two objects in view:—

Firstly, I have endeavoured to take as broad a view as possible of the whole position so as to present a sketch in which the various aspects of the problem are presented in their correct perspective.

Secondly, I have tried to express my ideas in simple language so that they may be readily followed by the ordinary reader who has not perhaps the time or the inclination to tackle the more serious text-books.

It is not perhaps generally realised that the nineteenth and twentieth centuries are witnessing a financial revolution, none the less important because it is being effected without bloodshed and almost without it being realised that a revolution is in progress. I refer to the disappearance of gold as a medium of currency and exchange and its replacement by paper of one kind or another—bank notes, commercial bills, cheques and similar devices. It is becoming increasingly evident that the methods of control applicable to the older system are no longer effective with the new, and it would appear that certain parts of the theory of Economics will have to be re-written or at least considerably modified.

In developing the subject I have made free use of existing economic theory as set forth in the writings of recognised authorities on the subject. In so far as I have modified or departed from orthodox theory I have endeavoured to justify the views which I have set forth, and I venture to hope that the results arrived at will not be found to be unreasonable.

In order that the reader should be able to understand the causes which underly the present crisis and the misfortunes to which it has given birth, it is necessary that he should know something of the working of the industrial and financial machine which controls the destinies of mankind and incidentally the lives of millions of individuals who may be thrown out of employment by any failure in its operations.

I propose to begin, therefore, by describing certain factors which have assumed importance during the present crisis, and I shall then endeavour to explain, in the light of these general principles, how this disaster has come about. It must not be supposed, however, that this brief survey is a complete abridged theory of Economics. Many branches of the subject will be passed over, not because they are without importance, but simply because they do not appear to be relevant to the present investigation.

THE HUMAN FACTOR

Political Economy or Economics has been defined as a "study of men's actions in ordinary business life; thus it is on one side a study of wealth, and on the other, and more important side, a part of the study of man."(1)

Modern theories of Economics, which may be said to have been evolved from the earlier theories of Political Economy, have a somewhat narrower scope, but the human factor still remains of fundamental importance.

It is of course the aim of economists to devise rules which will help to explain the course of events, and serve as a guide to future conduct, and these rules are often expressed in the form of algebraical formulae or geometrical diagrams. Unfortunately the interpretation of actual events in terms of these formulae is a matter of considerable difficulty and involves a large amount of detailed argument and discussion, and this mass of detail tends to obscure the nature of the foundations on which the whole structure is erected.

The earnest student of economic problems must therefore guide his frail barque between Scylla and Charybdis. On the one hand he must take care that he does not commit himself to theories which are logically inconsistent and which raise hopes which are impossible of realisation. On the other hand he must see that he is not engulfed in a whirlpool of formulae and statistics, which may be logically correct, but which are justified only in so far as the premises on which they are founded are in agreement with the facts which they are designed to interpret.

It would be unreasonable to suggest that economists are not alive to the fact that economic theory is based on certain assumptions as to human conduct, but it may certainly be said that the assumptions which are made as to business customs and the interpretations which are placed on human motives, do not usually stand out with that clearness which their significance would render desirable.

It must further be remembered that human conduct is influenced by many factors which alter with the lapse of time, and groups of individuals may not react to economic forces to-day in the same way which they might have done a few years ago. Due weight must be attached to considerations of this sort.

THE VERIFICATION OF ECONOMIC THEORIES

In scientific investigations it is an accepted principle that theories should be tested and re-tested by comparing them with the facts which it is their purpose to explain. Unfortunately the testing of economic theories in this fashion is by no means so simple as the testing of theories in the physical sciences. The subject has received a great deal of attention at the hands of professional economists, but the most zealous worker in this field would hardly contend that matters had as yet been established on a satisfactory basis.

It is easy to write down equations connecting the various quantities which form the basis of any economic theory, and it is not difficult to ensure the formal correctness of the equations by a suitable adjustment of the definitions. It is when an attempt is made to identify the quantities which appear in the equations with anything which can be measured in real life that the trouble begins.

It would be quite beyond the scope of the present essay to attempt a detailed discussion of these difficulties, and anyone who is interested in this particular aspect of the matter can find ample illustrations in any text-book on Economics.

I will content myself with observing that, although the difficulties are very real, definite progress has been made, and is still being made, towards an understanding of the various factors underlying the alternate booms and depressions which disturb the regular flow of industrial life. If further progress is to be made it is essential that these efforts should be continued.

It is also well to remember that pure theory can provide appropriate labels for the various conceptions which enter into a discussion and it can ensure that these labels are so devised that the whole scheme is logically consistent in itself, but it cannot determine facts. The appropriate and essential facts must be determined by an appeal to experience in each particular case.

REFERENCES

In making a brief survey of a very large subject it is not always possible to give adequate reasons in support of every statement which is made in the course of the argument, and it has therefore been found desirable to include a certain number of references which will enable the reader, if he so wishes, to fill in the inevitable gaps in the text.

The list of references must be regarded from this standpoint and must not be taken as a bibliography of the whole subject. I need hardly say that such a compilation would occupy a vastly greater amount of space than that which I have felt justified in allotting to it.

CHAPTER II

THE CONTROL OF INDUSTRIAL OUTPUT

THE CUSTOMER'S RIGHT OF FREE CHOICE

In a state which is governed on thorough-going communistic principles a customer who complains that the goods displayed for his selection in a government shop are lacking in variety, is no doubt thrown into prison as a just reward for his temerity. The problem of adjusting supply to meet demand is naturally simplified by making it illegal for the customer to demand what the government is unable to supply.

In more civilised communities on the other hand every citizen has the right to spend his money in whatever way may seem best to him, and this right is so much a part of our daily lives that the average man scarcely realises its existence. Still less does he appreciate the consequences which follow from this apparently simple custom.

The next time the reader enters a shop let him take a glance round, and let him make a rough estimate in his own mind of the number of different items which are offered for sale, or if he wishes to carry out his investigation in his own home let him take the price list of any shop and count the items in the index.

If the shop is a small one the items will probably

be numbered in hundreds, but if it is a large one they will certainly be numbered in thousands. Next it must be remembered that there are many different kinds of shop and that each type of shop has its own separate lists of items. Taking it all in all we shall err on the side of caution if we say that articles in fairly common use are to be numbered in tens of thousands.

It is often stated that a good salesman, who cannot supply what is asked for, can persuade the customer to buy something else, but the extent to which this sort of thing is possible must be strictly limited. A customer who asks for tea is not likely to be satisfied with sugar or cheese, and a customer who requires a new pair of trousers is unlikely to be tempted by an offer of a pair of boots or a new hat.

It would I think be unreasonable to weary the reader with further argument on the same lines, but the importance of this matter cannot be over-emphasised. The customer's freedom of choice is one of the corner-stones of the industrial edifice, and a clear grasp of this fundamental fact and its consequences is necessary for a proper appreciation of the structure which rests upon it.

PREDICTING DEMAND

It is the business of the commercial community to supply the needs of the customer, and competition between different firms and different individuals is usually sufficiently keen to ensure that the service shall be efficiently carried out.

One of the factors in this complex problem has already been referred to, that is to say the extraordinary variety of articles which traders and industrialists are expected to supply.

The second factor which has to be taken into consideration, and which complicates the problem facing the business man, is the time which elapses between the collection of the raw material and the final production of the finished article. Several months must elapse between seed time and harvest, and enough grain must be stored to tide over the period between one harvest and the next. It is also evident that a certain margin is necessary to provide for bad seasons when the crops are exceptionally small.

Again, in the case of manufactured goods, the raw materials must often be collected from the ends of the earth, and must be transported to the factory. In the factory itself they pass through a number of operations, and they must then be finally transported to some shop within easy reach of the actual purchaser. All this takes time.

The upshot of the matter is that production has to commence some six to eighteen months before the article can be displayed before the potential customer, and it is therefore necessary for the business man to make an estimate of what consumption is likely to be some six to eighteen months in advance.

It is this estimate which determines output and not the actual consumption at the time the goods are produced.

Now in the interval, while goods are in the course of manufacture, the appearance of the scene may alter. For one reason or another the customer's requirements may change, and the predictions may be falsified.

THE CUSTOMER'S REQUIREMENTS

The dictates of fashion are notoriously fickle, and some changes in the customer's demands may be entirely capricious. Other changes in the demand for commodities may be due to new discoveries, to political developments and other fortuitous causes. But the most important changes in demand are not those which are associated with factors of this type, they are those which are due to economic factors, and as such they demand special consideration.

The most important factor affecting the demands of any group of individuals is spending power, and this in turn may be affected by unemployment, by changes in rates of wages and salaries, and by changes in retail prices.

Nor are we entitled to assume that the demand for any particular commodity is proportional to the spending power of potential consumers. A man cannot wear two pairs of boots, and it is unlikely that he will wish to wear two hats. Therefore reduced spending power will mean that he will probably try to make his boots and hats last longer, but increased spending power may mean that he will demand boots and hats of better quality, or he may even economise on shoe leather and purchase a motor-car.

Again it may be found that financial or economic disturbances involve the transfer of spending power from one group of individuals to another, and it is clearly to be expected that such alterations in the distribution of spending power will also involve corresponding changes in the demands for commodities.

Much more might be written in the same strain, but enough has I think been said to show that the problem of foreseeing and supplying the customer's needs is by no means a simple one.

THE CONTROL OF INVESTMENT

The previous section has referred to the problem of controlling production, and reference must now be made to another problem which is even more important and even more difficult.

Most of the commodities which are required in the modern world involve some form of capital expenditure for their production. Irrigation schemes are required for growing cotton, mines are needed in order to obtain the materials which are buried in the bowels of the earth, factories and machinery are required for the final shaping of finished products, and so on, and it is one of the paradoxes of modern industry that the cheaper the article the more elaborate is the machinery which is usually required in order to make it. Thus a box of matches which sells for a penny has involved in its manufacture hundreds of separate operations, and has called for the use of machinery worth many thousands of pounds.

Now the development of all this machinery of production is not a matter of months but of years, and it involves the expenditure of large sums of money and a large amount of human effort. Still more it involves the training of large numbers of men who are specially skilled in the production of this kind of machinery and who are probably ill fitted for any other form of employment.

And there is yet another point. Commodities which are produced in excess of the normal demand are usually saleable at a reduced price, but with fixed capital this is very seldom the case. A copper mine is of no value if the world demands tin or zinc, and factories and machines are seldom of much value for any purpose other than those for which they were originally designed. Mistakes are therefore extremely expensive. The money, or the human effort if we prefer to call it so, which has been expended in their construction has been almost entirely wasted. Further there usually remains the difficult problem of disposing of the workmen by absorbing them in other industries.

It is not too much to say that the wise control of

investment is one of the most vital and at the same time one of the most difficult problems of modern industry.

THE DIVISION OF LABOUR

The high standard of living which prevails at the present time is rendered possible by what is called the division of labour, the system under which each worker is allotted a small but highly specialised task. (2)

Unfortunately the specialised training which is necessary for each individual worker makes it very difficult to transfer workers from one industry to another, and the whole system is slow to adapt itself to changing conditions. Unemployment is often concentrated therefore in a few industries which may be entirely idle while other forms of employment are not seriously affected. Industries concerned with the production of machines for the use of other industries are particularly liable to be affected in this way. Trade depression may cause only a moderate reduction of business in the primary industry, but nobody wants new machines when existing machines are not being fully utilised, so that for the time being machine-makers are thrown completely out of employment.

All these things are necessary consequences of the customer's freedom of choice.

It is clearly unthinkable, however, that any progressive state should try to deprive the individual consumer of this right to spend his money as he thinks fit, and it is necessary therefore to accept the customer's right of choice as one of the conditions which the industrial structure must be prepared to comply with. All that can be done is to accept this factor as inevitable and take steps to meet it as best we may.

When the complexity of the problem is once realised the wonder is, not that mistakes are sometimes made, but that mistakes are not more frequent and more serious than is actually the case.

CHAPTER III

THE MARKET PLACE

AN OLD-FASHIONED MARKET

THERE are not many markets of the old-fashioned type to be found nowadays, for most things are sold at fixed prices in shops and stores. Nevertheless the spirit of the market place pervades the whole world of trade and industry and it is necessary to understand its influence.

Let us picture then some old market town to which farmers bring their fruit and vegetables, their chickens and their eggs, and let us visit the scene and watch the market in progress.

If we chat with the buyers and sellers we shall no doubt find that their actions are dictated by two main ideas. Firstly they will start on their bargaining with a definite idea as to the value of the article which they are trying to buy or sell. If the demand for any article is just about equal to the supply, bargains will be concluded at in or about this basic price.

At the same time buyers and sellers will be on the lookout for any inequality between demand and supply and will hasten to take advantage of it. If the demand is in excess of available supplies the sellers will probably succeed in charging a little more than the basic price. On the other hand if buyers are few sellers will be glad to take a little less to avoid having their wares left unsold. When there is free competition between buyers and sellers, therefore, the price level, demand and supply are all more or less elastic, and adjust themselves to the conditions prevailing at the moment.

It will be noticed that the seller who has obtained more than the basic price will consider that he has made a profit, whereas if he has accepted less than the basic price he will consider that he has done his marketing at a loss. This idea of profit and loss is accentuated when collection and distribution are carried out by middlemen. The income of these traders depends on the difference between the prices at which they buy and sell respectively, and small variations in price therefore assume an exaggerated importance.

As regards what has been called above the "basic price," we may in most cases regard it simply as the average price which has prevailed in recent markets. The important feature of the whole business is the elasticity of the price level and the way in which it responds to the bargaining power of buyer and seller respectively.

BARGAINING POWER

The influence which bargaining power exerts upon the price level has already been referred to in our description of the market in the previous section.

A shortage of supplies gives an advantage to the

seller and enables him to raise prices, while the existence of supplies in excess of the purchasers' needs causes sellers to lower prices in the hope that they will thus be enabled to dispose of the surplus.

The influence of bargaining power in economic problems is by no means confined, however, to straightforward cases of supply and demand. It can be traced in many other less obvious examples, and may influence the standard of living of whole nations and world-wide industries.

An industry, such as agriculture, which is in the hands of innumerable small producers, badly organised and often separated from one another by differences of race and language, is at a permanent disadvantage. Not only are profits small and uncertain, but the whole scale of wages and salaries is on a lower scale than in the case of other industries which are more favourably situated. At the other extreme may be noted a highly specialised and well-organised industry, such as the manufacture of motor-cars, which not only shows good profits but is able at the same time to pay high wages.

Again, history contains many examples of nations which have secured the advantages of some trade monopoly and have benefited accordingly. In the nineteenth century, for example, Great Britain was a pioneer in the engineering industry and in the manufacture of cotton fabrics, and she was thus enabled to secure in these trades a virtual monopoly which endured for several decades.

This position enabled her to adopt a standard of living in advance of the general standard of living existing in other countries, and the cost of this improved standard of living was no doubt accepted at the time as a legitimate part of the basic cost of the commodities which she was in a position to sell.

MONEY AS A COMMODITY

In discussing the progress of the market we have followed the usual custom and dealt with the prices of commodities in terms of money. It is equally correct however to regard money as a commodity and refer to its value in terms of other commodities. This alternative method of expression is important because it emphasises the fact that it is the balance, or lack of balance, between the supply of money and the supply of commodities which is the essential factor in determining prices, and it is just as important to consider the one as it is to consider the other.

THE QUANTITY OF MONEY IN THE MARKET

In comparing money to a commodity, however, it is necessary to remark that there exists, in addition to a large measure of similarity, one important difference. Sellers may hold commodities for a short time when prices are bad in order to secure better prices, but commodities which are for sale are generally useless to the seller, and in the long run they must be sold.

On the other hand people will hold up money for short or long periods from entirely different motives. Mrs. A may put by a shilling a week to buy a turkey at Christmas, or Mrs. B may put a shilling a week into the savings bank in order to provide for her old age, and these actions are not likely to be affected by the course of prices in the market.

What happens to Mrs. A's money which is temporarily withdrawn from the market or to Mrs. B's money which finds a home in the savings bank is another story to which we shall return in due course. The point of immediate interest is that the money is withdrawn from the market and plays no part in the transactions of the market place. The general principle, which is illustrated in this example, is that the quantity of money which enters the market, and which must be considered in determining price levels, is the amount which people decide or think they can afford to spend, and not the amount of money which they possess or which they can obtain by borrowing or otherwise.

It may of course happen that attractive prices induce a little more spending than would otherwise have taken place, but this does not affect the essential principle. It is known that saving does take place even in apparently adverse circumstances, and it must therefore be accepted as a fact that saving is governed by motives which are little affected by market fluctuations.

CHAPTER IV

COMMERCIAL MOTIVES

TRADE AND INDUSTRY

MODERN commerce involves two main types of activity, the business of transforming raw materials into finished products or into intermediate products which form the raw material of some other industry, and the business of distributing these products to the consumer or to the next factory as the case may be. The former is the province of the manufacturer, and the latter the province of the trader.

In many cases particular firms or particular individuals combine both functions. More especially is this the case when raw materials pass through a number of distinct stages before reaching their final form. In such cases the manufacturer is only strictly a manufacturer in respect of the work which he himself carries out. As regards his stock of raw materials, his goods in process and his stock of completed articles his position is the position of a trader.

Nevertheless, in spite of some uncertainty as to the exact position of individuals, it is convenient to preserve the distinction between trader and manufacturer, since there is a difference in the motives which operate in the two types of business.

THE TRADER

The trader buys his commodities at a certain price, incurs certain expenses in storing and transporting them, and finally sells them again. He determines his position by calculating the cost of storage and the cost of transport, he adds to this the interest on his working capital and an amount to represent the remuneration of himself and his personal staff, and arrives at a final figure which may be called his basic selling price.

If he is able to sell at more than this figure he considers that he has made a profit, if at less then he has made a loss.

The trader is essentially a worker in the market place. He has little fixed capital and his whole business is elastic; profit and loss dominate his horizon, and he will expand or contract his business according as he foresees a profit or a loss.

THE MANUFACTURER

The position of the manufacturer is somewhat different. He owns a factory or factories representing a considerable amount of fixed capital, divided probably into shares and debentures. In addition to this he controls a staff of trained workmen and officials which it has probably taken him years to collect, train and organise.

His aim is to show as large a return as possible on

his share capital, but in the last resort he will endeavour to prevent the closing down of his factory and the dispersal of his staff. His attitude will be that it is better that the shareholders should suffer the loss of a few years' dividends rather than that the business should collapse, and that they should lose the whole of their money.

THE INVESTOR

When an existing factory is working to its full capacity the question naturally arises as to whether it is desirable to extend it so as to provide for a larger output. Or again some new process may be under consideration and the question at issue is whether it is worth while to erect a factory for its development.

In either case a statement is prepared showing the estimated working costs on one side and the estimated receipts on the other. If this account shows that the estimated receipts are in excess of the estimated costs, then the enterprise is considered to be profitable, and the construction of the new factory will probably be put in hand. If on the other hand the costs appear to form the larger total then the scheme will be abandoned.

The position of the investor is therefore very similar to the position of the trader. He will embark on new business if he foresees a profit, but not otherwise.

PROFIT AND LOSS

We have defined profit as the difference between cost and selling price.

So far as selling price is concerned the figure which is involved in this definition is fairly easily arrived at, but on the costing side the matter is not quite so simple, and the word "profit" is actually used in a variety of different meanings.

In a machine shop for example there will be direct labour charges which can be allocated at once to the particular articles concerned, and there will be the wages of the foreman and storekeepers and perhaps others which must be distributed over the whole of the output of that particular shop. Finally there will be the manager, the accounting staff and others whose salaries or wages must be distributed over the whole factory, and so on.

In business accounts therefore we meet such expressions as "direct costs," "indirect costs," "gross profit," "net profit" and the like. In such accounts interest on capital (other than debenture interest) is not usually included in the costs, but it appears as part of the "profits."

In discussions on Economics it is usual to regard the interest on all invested capital as a part of the costs, and yet another meaning is therefore attached to the word "profit." To avoid confusion this kind of profit may be called the "economic profit."

It is the hope of making a profit in the economic

sense which encourages the trader and the investor to expand their enterprises. It is this hope in fact which is the mainspring of the whole commercial machine, the driving power which keeps the wheels of industry in motion. Withdraw the hope of profit and trade languishes and investment comes to a standstill. (3)

Having reached this important conclusion, however, it may be well, even at this early stage of our investigation, to sound a note of warning. The economic system must operate in such a way as to offer the trader and the investor a reasonable hope of profit, or these necessary contributors to the welfare of the community will not perform their functions, and business will be hampered accordingly. On the other hand it is necessary that excessive profits should be avoided or business will be unduly stimulated and enterprises will be started which are unsound in themselves and which must ultimately result in failure. When everyone is making profits nobody pauses to enquire whether a particular enterprise is sound or not. Steady progress is not attained by such methods.

The industrial machine is a delicately balanced piece of mechanism, which requires for its proper working that each component should fulfil its proper function and no more. Putting aside the question as to whether such an ideal is attainable in practice, it may be said that the proper working of the industrial machine requires that the trader should be able to foresee a modest profit. If excessive profits are being made money will be wasted, whereas if there are no profits to be made trade will languish and workers will be thrown out of employment.

CHAPTER V

MASS PRODUCTION

THE EFFICIENCY OF LABOUR

FROM the very earliest times mankind has tried to increase the efficiency of its labour by the use of tools.

In these earlier efforts progress was restricted by the amount of muscular energy which a man was able to bring to bear upon his task, and a great stride forward was made when the invention of the steam engine enabled this limitation to be removed. (4)

Output has been still further increased by the invention of machines which are capable of carrying out automatically operations which had previously been controlled by human skill, and complex machines have also been developed which carry out a succession of separate operations without the need for any independent human control. (5)

As a result of these developments the efficiency of labour has steadily increased during the nineteenth and twentieth centuries, nor is there as yet any signs of finality.

Some years ago a somewhat different aspect of the problem received a good deal of attention. The movements of the workman were studied by experts, and methods were devised for carrying out each operation with the minimum of human effort.

Workmen were then given detailed instructions, based on the conclusions of the experts, as to how each operation should be carried out. (6)

More recently attention has been directed towards questions of organisation, such as grouping of factories and the allotment of work between different groups. Arrangements of this character are generally referred to as "rationalisation."

I do not propose to discuss these various methods in greater detail since the general effect on the industrial situation is the same. They all tend to increase the efficiency of labour, or in other words they reduce the amount of labour which is necessary in order to secure a given output of commodities. During the past two decades the increase of the efficiency of labour is estimated at about 50 per cent, or more than 2 per cent per annum. (7)

NEW INDUSTRIES

There is no better example of the advantages of mass production than the development of the motor industry. We are here dealing with the evolution of a new method of transport, and of new human wants which have been aroused by these new possibilities.

Owing to the use of mass production methods the price of a motor-car at the present time is less than a quarter of the price which had to be paid for a similar or perhaps inferior car a few years ago. This remarkable improvement in value has attracted a number of purchasers who would otherwise have spent their money elsewhere, so that reductions in price have attracted more money from the public instead of less.

The rapid expansion of wireless broadcasting is another example of the way in which mass production methods assist in the development of a new industry.

The steady improvement in electric lighting is yet another but perhaps less spectacular example. The electric lamp which is sold to the public for a few shillings conceals within its simple glass bulb a romance of scientific and technical achievement far surpassing any fable of the Arabian Nights. It is the success of these methods which has conferred important benefits on the community at large, and which has at the same time provided employment for thousands of workers. I need hardly add that the commercial production of electric lamps by other than mass production methods would be entirely impossible.

ESTABLISHED INDUSTRIES

In the previous section reference has been made to new industries which are being developed to meet the expanding demand which they have themselves created for their own products.

It is obvious, however, that the condition of affairs which has been pictured cannot be a permanent one. A man cannot wear two pairs of boots and he cannot drive two motor-cars. Sooner or later the market becomes saturated and demand approaches a limit.

If an industry is dealing with an established and presumably saturated market improved methods of production are not likely to attract more money from the public. On the contrary the public will buy what it needs at the reduced prices and will therefore spend less money than before on that particular commodity. In such cases mass production methods will reduce employment instead of increasing it.

THE NET RESULT

It is sometimes argued that Rationalisation is a cure for unemployment. (8) On the other hand it is often believed, particularly by the workers, that mass production in any of its various forms tends to throw people out of employment. It is well that we should have clear ideas on this matter, and the truth is not I think far to seek.

In new industries reductions in price increase the demand to such an extent that the increased output induces the consumer to spend more money than he would have otherwise, and employment is increased. In existing industries on the other hand the demand is less elastic and increased efficiency probably causes a reduction of employment.

The development of mass production methods has therefore two distinct and opposite effects on employment according as it is applied to old or new industries respectively. The ideal situation would arise if the loss of employment in one type of industry could always be balanced by gains in others. Unfortunately it is not easy to suggest means by which the creation of new industries may be artificially stimulated. The most that can be done is to create a favourable atmosphere. Nor is it easy to control reductions in industries in which the demand for labour is decreasing. The remedy which naturally suggests itself is that the displacement of workers in established industries should be controlled, and this idea has been put forward repeatedly during the past century by politicians and social reformers. The difficulties and dangers of such a policy are however all too evident.

The recent failure of the attempt to restrict the output of rubber is a familiar example of the futility of individual attempts at the restriction of output. Restriction of output is only possible when all producers can be brought into the scheme and held effectively to their undertakings. Any individual nation which persists in using obsolete methods must inevitably be driven out of business by foreign competition. If any restriction of progress by an individual nation is to be permissible it can only be so in very special circumstances and for a very limited period of time.

As regards the possibility of international agreements it is of course impossible to express a definite opinion. It can only be said that increasing experience and knowledge of human nature tends to decrease one's faith in the efficiency of such instruments.

THE REDUCED NEED FOR TECHNICAL SKILL

In addition to securing increased efficiency modern efforts in the design of machinery also tend towards making the machines themselves more and more "foolproof." The earlier types of any machine usually suffer from minor defects of design which demand the attention of a skilful and intelligent workman, but experience gradually enables these difficulties to be overcome. Eventually a type of machine is evolved which can be operated by workers without either high intelligence or high technical skill. Such a machine only requires occasional technical attention in order to keep it in repair.

This tendency in machine design is of profound and fundamental importance, and its significance is not always fully realised. It means that many industries which have hitherto been the monopoly of Europeans are now capable of being worked by Africans and Asiatics who have at present a much lower standard of living. The British textile industry is an outstanding example, and the ultimate fate of that industry is by no means obvious.

AGRICULTURE

Although it is hardly a field for mass production methods in the ordinary sense, the agricultural industry has also experienced the effects of the general striving after efficiency, for the introduction of tractors and various new types of farm machinery has considerably reduced the amount of labour which is necessary in order to secure a given output.

Agricultural output has also been increased indirectly in a way which was not, I think, foreseen until it actually took place. On the contrary nineteenth-century scientists who were rash enough to enter upon the task of prophecy predicted a shortage of food rather than a surplus.

What has actually happened is that motor-cars and tractors driven by internal-combustion engines have replaced horses as a means of transport over short distances, and as a source of power on the farm itself. Land which was formerly employed in supplying forage and grain for horses is no longer required for that purpose therefore, and has become available for the growing of other agricultural products. For the moment there is too much land under cultivation, and a surplus of agricultural commodities.

Men trained in agricultural pursuits do not readily adapt themselves to other occupations, and for this and other reasons the control of agricultural output is a difficult if not insuperable problem.

CHAPTER VI

THE DISTRIBUTION OF WEALTH

WHAT IS WEALTH?

A MAN may be considered wealthy either because he has a large income, or because he has great possessions, and a rigid analysis would take both types of wealth into consideration.

Many forms of capital, such as factories and machinery, are valued simply as a means of producing other things, and their value is measured by the income which they are expected to earn in such production. Other forms of capital, such as houses, are of value in themselves, but are often rented by the owner to the user so that once more the rent or income becomes the generally accepted measure of their value. Rare pictures or china on the other hand may be said to be valuable in themselves independently of their power of earning income, but such exceptions form a very small proportion of the whole wealth of the country and need not be further considered in a sketch which is merely intended to exhibit the broad features of economic theory.

Passing by such minor details therefore we may regard income as wealth, and the distribution of the national wealth becomes the distribution of the national income, or, as it is sometimes called, the national dividend.

THE DISTRIBUTION OF THE NATIONAL DIVIDEND

When a man receives money he is able to purchase with it an equivalent amount of commodities, or in other words he becomes entitled to a certain portion of the national dividend. It is necessary therefore to consider how it is that these claims to a portion of the national dividend are determined, and how they are affected by various factors economic and financial; questions as to how the claims have arisen need not concern us for the moment.

For our immediate purpose the more important claims to a share of the national dividend may be regarded as of four distinct types, and the typical claimants may be called wage-earners, pensioners, bondholders and shareholders respectively.

Salaries and rates of wages are fixed by custom or agreement. It has been pointed out by some economists that the wages paid to a skilled artisan represent in part true wages and in part a return upon the capital invested in the artisan's training. (9) Such considerations assume importance for certain purposes, but they need not be considered here.

The pensioner class is one which has assumed an increasing importance during recent years, and pensions have been granted by the government to ex-soldiers, to wage-earners who have reached a certain age and to wage-earners who have been injured in the course of their employment. The amount of the pension is usually fixed and is intended to remain unaltered during the pensioner's lifetime. In times of difficulty, however, the rate of pension may be revised by the government either upwards or downwards.

Bonds and shares are different forms of investment, and may be distinguished from each other by the different way in which the income upon them is arrived at.

Government loans are representative of the former type, which for our present purpose may be taken to include rent, mortgages, debenture interest and in fact any form of security yielding a fixed rate of interest.

The return on share capital on the other hand depends on the earnings of the enterprise in which the capital is invested. The element of risk thus enters into the transaction and differentiates the shareholder's rights very sharply from those of the other groups already referred to.

Government loans are not always free from risk, and commercial enterprises may be so firmly established that they possess a high degree of security, so that it is convenient to regard each individual investment as made up of two parts, one part having the characteristics of a bond, and the other part the characteristics of a share.

The return which the shareholder obtains on his money is of course compared by him with the return obtained by the bondholder, and in fact the shareholder naturally considers that he is entitled to at least as much return as the bondholder is. This idea is expressed by saying that an enterprise which is earning more than the normal rate of interest is making a profit, and an enterprise which is earning less than the normal rate of interest is being run at a loss.

THE FACTORS WHICH INFLUENCE THE DISTRIBUTION OF THE NATIONAL DIVIDEND

In war-time large sums of money are borrowed by belligerent governments probably at high rates of interest, and the bondholders claim rises accordingly. The reactions which are called forth by such conditions will be described in Chapter XV.

In more normal times the distribution of the national dividend between the various groups may be said to be the result of custom which in its turn is largely influenced by the bargaining power of the particular group concerned.

Apart from custom, however, the distribution is powerfully affected by economic factors, and these factors are of special importance when short period fluctuations are under consideration. There are three such factors which need our attention, namely, the total volume of output, the level of prices and the level of costs.

If trade expands and the national output is increased, it is evident that employment will increase also, and in this way the wage-earner obtains a portion of the increased output. He may also obtain a further advantage owing to the fact that a demand for labour tends to raise wages.

The bondholder and the pensioner benefit very little from increased output, although they may gain slightly through decreased taxation. The shareholder on the other hand finds that his fixed charges, as he calls the bondholder's portion, are now spread over a larger output and that he is getting the benefit of reduced costs, and this in turn means increased profits.

Even apart from a reduction in the proportion of fixed charges, a larger output enables a factory to be run more efficiently, and here again increased output means larger profits.

Finally we come to the question of the price level, and here we find that wage-earners, pensioners and bondholders form one group and shareholders another. A rise in prices causes no change in the amount of money to which members of the first group are entitled either as wages or as interest, but it reduces the number of things which they can buy with the money, so that their real share of the national dividend has diminished in exact proportion to the increase in the price level. The shareholder on the other hand has benefited from the rise in prices to the exact extent to which the others have lost. Conversely, if prices fall, the shareholder loses and all the other members of the community reap the benefit.

The position of the pensioner and the bondholder is particularly interesting. According to the letter of the law their claims are absolute, and, like Shylock in *The Merchant of Venice*, they are entitled to their pound of flesh whatever may happen to their less fortunate fellows. They might well become entitled to the whole of the national dividend, leaving no balance available for either wage-earner or shareholder.

TAXATION

Taxes may be of such a character that they are paid more or less impartially by the whole population or they may be of such a character that they are paid almost entirely by one particular class. The income tax for example is paid almost entirely by the two groups which have been called above bondholders and shareholders, and it leaves wage-earners and pensioners almost untouched. Changes in taxation may therefore give rise to corresponding changes in the distribution of the national dividend and the government of the day has therefore considerable power to influence the position.

Again, the principal items of government expenditure are wages, salaries and pensions on the one hand and the payment of interest on the national debt on the other, and the amounts which are devoted to each of these purposes exercise an obvious effect on the distribution of wealth between the various people concerned.

THE ACTIVITY OF TRADE

The actual distribution of wealth is evidently affected by a large number of different influences, but the question which concerns us more particularly in our present investigation is the relationship between profits and the activity of trade.

Improving trade means greater output, more employment and lower cost. Increasing employment means in its turn that demand will tend to outrun the supply and prices will tend to rise. Greater trade activity involves therefore greater output, lower costs and higher prices, and all these three factors combine to increase the shareholder's portion of the national dividend, that is to say they increase his profits.

On the other hand declining trade reduces the shareholder's portion and turns his profits into losses.

THE EFFECT OF TRADE LOSSES

Nobody is likely to raise any objections if his portion of the national dividend is increased, but any tendency to reduce his share calls forth certain reactions which must now be considered. Of these reactions the effect on trade is the most important.

The attitude of the trader and the manufacturer, who represent the shareholders' interests, has already been discussed. Their aim is to make profits, or, if the worst comes to the worst, to avoid losses. If trade and industry become unprofitable they will reduce their business, and wage-earners will be thrown out of employment.

The reduction in employment reduces output and leads to a further reduction of the shareholder's portion, so that the whole train of events is cumulative in its effects. Obviously such a condition of affairs cannot continue indefinitely or the whole economic structure would collapse, and ultimately other factors must make their appearance which enable the shareholder to make his profits once more, and trade and industry then begin to recover. These factors will be discussed in Chapter IX.

One thing is clear—unless the trader and the industrialist are able to make modest profits, the industrial machine will not work.

THE QUESTION OF SAVING AND INVESTMENT

The money which is made available by the savings of the thrifty is the life blood of trade and industry. It enables the wastage caused by wear and tear to be renewed and provides the means which are necessary for further progress.

Thrift is not confined to any particular class of society, but it is obvious that the well-to-do are in a better position to save a part of their income than those who are less fortunately situated, so that savings are mainly derived from those groups of citizens which have been described as bondholders and shareholders.

Trade and industry will stagnate if there is a lack

of money available for investment just as surely as if there is a lack of profit. The question arises therefore as to whether, in any particular case, slackness of trade is due to lack of money; and the question takes a very practical form during a trade slump such as exists at the present time.

Since the restoration of trade and industry demands that traders should be given back their profits, it is necessary to consider whether measures should be designed in such a way that the shareholder's position is improved at the expense of the wage-earner or the bondholder or both. If the bondholder is squeezed too hard trade may be hampered just as surely as by lack of profits, and for this reason many economists have suggested that a reduction of wages would be the best way of stimulating trade.

The proposal requires examination from several angles, but on the question of savings, it is an observed fact that most trade slumps lead eventually to an abundant supply of money which is available for investment, and, so long as this is the case, it would appear that the bondholder's rights are still capable of some reduction without seriously affecting the welfare of the community. A similar conclusion may also be arrived at on somewhat different grounds. (10)

The problem of restoring trade and industry after a slump is obviously a difficult one, but the line of argument indicated above would certainly appear to suggest the measures intended to restore the shareholder's profits should be designed to do so at the expense of the bondholder rather than the wage-earner or the pensioner, but subject to the condition that there remains an adequate supply of cheap funds to provide for the legitimate requirements of trade and industry.

CHAPTER VII

MONEY

FORMS OF MONEY

In early days money consisted of coins or tokens, and its purpose was to facilitate the barter of commodities. In the modern world money takes various forms and serves various purposes.

The most important forms of money at the present time are coins, currency notes, bank money and gold. All these serve the same purposes as the coinage and may be regarded as equivalent to it.

Bank money is a comparatively modern development, and is of very great interest and importance. The essence of the system is that a depositor hands over cash to his bank and receives in return, not cash, but the right to demand cash. Now it is clear that if A owes B one hundred pounds, and B owes C the same amount, and C owes D, and D owes A, then the whole affair can be settled quite simply by handing round "a right to demand cash." The actual cash need not appear in the transactions at all.

Subject to the condition that overdrafts must not exceed deposits a banker can settle any number of business debts in this fashion without any cash at all. Provided that his customers remain solvent he has the power of creating, and does in fact create, the means of paying off as many debts as his customers may ask him to settle for them.

Loans and investments are closely allied to money, but they are not cash, and possess their own distinct functions and properties. They will be dealt with in due course.

SUPPLY AND DEMAND

Having agreed that money may be dealt with like a commodity, we are in a position to consider the usual problems of the market place, that is to say, what determines the basic value of money and what special factors influence the forces of supply of demand.

It is convenient to commence our investigation by addressing ourselves to the second of these two questions.

The first idea that naturally takes shape in our minds may be expressed somewhat as follows. A certain quantity of money is in existence and is available for exchange against a certain quantity of commodities. Therefore the value of money will depend on the amount of money in existence. The more money there is the less it will be worth and *vice versa.*

Following this train of thought let us consider the attitude of mind of an ordinary tradesman whose business is paying its way and let us ask ourselves whether his actions are really influenced either by lack of cash or by a surplus of cash. If we put firmly on one side any ideas which may arise in our minds as to questions of credit, only one answer to this question seems possible. His most important transactions are settled by cheque and do not involve cash transactions at all. So far as cash is required his bank supplies his needs and absorbs any surplus which he does not require.

The conclusion to be drawn from this argument is quite definite. The supply of money is elastic and adjusts itself freely to the demand for it, and the volume of money in existence cannot possess any particular significance in relation to the price level.

A somewhat similar conclusion was reached in discussing the progress of events in the market place, and it was there suggested that the significant quantity is not the total amount of money but the amount of money which people decide to spend. Let us take this hint therefore and endeavour to picture the course of events in that larger market which may be supposed to include the whole of the national output.

HOARDING VERSUS SPENDING

Let us try to picture the whole of the national output as if it were collected into one shop and let us suppose that each commodity is marked with the selling price.

In the first instance let us consider a year in which the total prices marked on the commodities are exactly equal to the amount of money which has been paid out in wages and interest, and let us further assume that the various individuals to whom the money is handed over decide to spend the whole of it. Then it is clear that the whole position is in equilibrium and will remain so until something happens to disturb it.

Let us now vary our assumptions however. Starting with a year in which there is a balance between production and consumption, let us assume that in the following year a certain number of people decide to hoard their money instead of spending it. These people will buy less, and the quantity of commodities produced will therefore exceed the demand for them. Traders will try to dispose of their surplus stocks by reducing prices and the value of money in terms of commodities will rise.

To continue this story we may assume that the hoarders of money change their policy in the following year and spend, not only the money to which they are entitled for that year, but their hoarded surplus as well. In that case the previous condition of affairs will be reversed, prices will rise, and the value of money will fall.

Our excursion into the national market place has therefore yielded the same result as before. It is the volume of spending which is the essential quantity which must be studied when the value of money is under consideration.

THE SPENDERS OF MONEY

Before proceeding further with our discussion it may perhaps be well to explain that the word "spending" is used in this chapter, and indeed throughout the present essay, to convey the idea that goods are purchased and consumed so that it is in fact only another aspect of consumption. An individual buys food in order to eat it and he buys clothes in order to wear them. So far as economic theory is concerned commodities have completed their course through the industrial machine and fulfilled their destiny when they pass into the hands of the consumer.

Using the word "spending" in this sense, a manufacturer does not spend money when he pays his workmen. In return for the work done he gives his workmen so much money in the form of wages, and it is the workmen who spend the money and consume the commodities which they purchase therewith. The manufacturer can only "spend" the money which he retains as his personal share in the form of interest or salary.

Those who spend or control the spending of money may now be regarded as falling into five groups which I shall call wage-earners, traders, manufacturers, investors and the government, and the influence exerted by each of these groups must be separately considered.

Most wage-earners spend the whole of their incomes, so that the volume of their spending depends upon the amount of money which is given to them to spend. This depends in turn on two factors, the rate of wages and the number of employed. When trade is contracting the money rate of wages in competitive industries tends to fall, and, so far as spending power is concerned, tends to accentuate the effect of unemployment. The volume of employment does not depend upon the action of the workmen (except in the case of strikes) but upon the policy of traders, manufacturers and investors. The motives governing the actions of these groups have been discussed in Chapter IV and it is only necessary to summarise the position here.

Traders do not consume goods, but the effect of expanding trade is to increase retailers' stocks and goods in process, and this has the same effect as if the goods were bought and consumed. When trade is contracting on the other hand these stocks are released, and they must be deducted from the volume of spending proper in order to arrive at the volume of spending which is actually effective.

Manufacturers in their capacity as such do not consume commodities, but it is their business to make predictions as to the quantities of commodities which are likely to be required and their decisions affect the number of workmen which they employ. The spending of the wage-earners is affected accordingly.

The position of the investor may be looked at from two points of view. On the one hand he is the recipient of the money which is paid in respect of interest and profits, and on the other hand he is the source from which funds must be obtained in order to finance those new enterprises which are so essential for the progressive development of industry.

The well-to-do class to which investors may be assumed to belong differs in its habits from the wage-earning class already referred to. Individuals have a larger share of worldly wealth and are therefore in a position to save a portion of their income instead of spending it. Under all normal circumstances the well-to-do classes save a proportion of their income, the actual proportion being about 10 per cent. The money thus saved may be either invested or hoarded.

If the money saved is invested, that is to say if it is utilised for the development of new enterprises, the spending power which was represented by the money disappears, and new factories or whatever it may be take its place. The money has therefore been spent just as truly as if it had been spent on consumable commodities such as food or clothing. The immediate effect is the same although the ultimate result in the more distant future may be different.

Now it has already been pointed out that the motive which induces the investor to invest his money instead of hoarding it is the hope of making a profit. If conditions are bad he will be tempted to hoard it.

The trader's and the investor's hopes of making

profits arise in somewhat different ways and it does not necessarily follow that trade booms and investment booms will coincide, but general feelings of optimism or pessimism may well affect both simultaneously.

In a general way therefore a boom increases spending, reduces the value of money and raises prices, while a slump has the opposite effect. Unfortunately also the results tend to be cumulative. Increased spending increases demand and stimulates production, and increased production involves more employment and a further increase in spending power and so on. But that is another story which will be told in due course.

Finally we come to the position of the government, which possesses two powers of vital importance, namely the control of taxation and the control of the currency. Taken together these two powers give the government the power of spending money without having any money to spend! Without affecting the spending of individuals the government can pay its way by simply printing paper money, but the increased spending inevitably reduces the value of money itself. The further results of such a practice are unfortunately only too well known, and need no description here. (11)

THE BASIC VALUE OF MONEY

Prior to the Great War the currencies of the more important countries of the world were based on gold. Under this arrangement it is believed, and no doubt rightly believed, that the value of gold determines what I have called the basic value of money. The basic value of gold depends in its turn on the cost of production, but a discussion of the factors which go to influence the cost of production would be beyond the scope of the present essay.

Nor is it proposed to discuss here the basic value of paper money in a country which is not on the gold standard or something equivalent to it. This is a question of extreme difficulty which is at present imperfectly understood, and a discussion of such a topic would be quite foreign to our purpose.

It is sufficient to note that the value of gold does vary, and that the actual extent of the variations is known with sufficient accuracy to permit of effective discussion of the immediate issues. It may further be noted as an observed fact that a paper currency which is not upset by unsound government finance appears to possess a degree of stability at least equal to the stability of the gold standard. With these facts we must rest content.

CHAPTER VIII

SHORT TERM LOANS

CASH AND CREDIT

The essential characteristic of a short term loan is that it is readily convertible into cash at its face value. Although it occupies an intermediate position between money on the one hand and investment on the other, short term credit is more closely allied to money than it is to investment.

Investments can usually be sold, but they are not saleable at a fixed price, and for this reason the buying and selling of investments is not a convenient method of providing for the fluctuating demands of trade. In a normal way the spending power which a business can command consists of its cash plus the amount which it is able to borrow in the form of short term loans.

If trade is good and business is expanding, business men may decide to utilise both their cash and their credit resources in the development of business, and to this extent short term credits are equivalent to cash.

A connection is thus established, firstly between spending and cash, which is the right to spend, and secondly between cash and credit, which is the ability to borrow. In certain cases the ability to borrow determines the amount of spending, and the one may be regarded as equivalent to the other, but the identity is not universal, and confusion will arise unless credit, cash and spending are recognised as three separate entities each subject to its own laws and its own limitation. Nor is the situation rendered easier by the fact that the market for credit is described as the "Money Market," and cheap credit is commonly referred to as "cheap money."

The business of making short term loans is very largely in the hands of the banks, and the two parties to such transactions may be referred to as the bankers on the one hand and the traders and industrialists on the other.

THE POSITION OF THE BANKER

In modern countries the banking system usually consists of a central bank and what are termed member banks, and the central bank has powers which enable it to control the actions of the member banks, so that the whole system acts as if it were a single business. The mechanism by which this state of affairs is brought about need not concern us here.

A banker's primary duties are towards his depositors and his shareholders. His duty towards his depositors is to carry out his business in such a way as to avoid any risk of losing the depositors' money. His duty towards his shareholders is to earn interest on the bank's capital.

Short term loans play an important part in financing trade and industry, however, and a banker's secondary duties involve the making of loans in such a manner as to give trade and industry as much help as possible.

As regards his primary duties, the position is that cash provides a sure means of repaying the depositor, but it earns no interest. Investments on the other hand may earn interest but they are not always convertible into cash. Short term loans provide the exact type of security which the bank requires; they earn interest and at the same time they are continually turning into money as they fall due for repayment. A large proportion of a bank's assets are usually held in this form.

Experience has in fact fixed a certain proportion between cash, short term loans and investments which is found to give satisfactory results in practice, and this proportion is usually adhered to pretty closely.

It is a mistake to suppose therefore that the banks are inclined to restrict credit. On the contrary it is to their advantage to give as much credit as possible provided always that this can be done without undue risk. It is the failure of borrowers to repay the money when it falls due that causes the banks to take fright and restrict credit. And such failures may be traced back to errors which have been made by the trader in trying to predict the requirements of his customers.

Thus the present financial crisis was actually precipitated by the discovery that the assets of the

Austrian Bank known as the Credit Anstalt had fallen in value and that the bank had become insolvent. (12)

WORKING CAPITAL

The production of commodities takes time. Several months elapse between seed time and harvest, and there is further delay between the harvesting of the crop and the appearance of the final product on the table of the consumer. It is also necessary to provide for the consumer's demands between one harvest and the next. Similar considerations apply to all kinds of commodities. In each case the money which has been spent on production has disappeared, only to reappear again when the goods are sold to the final consumer. The value of half-finished goods, and the value of goods in transit and in stock, make up what is known as working capital.

Now the chief characteristic of working capital is that it offers a high degree of security. A particular consignment of goods may remain in the hands of a particular trader or manufacturer for a few weeks or a few months. At the end of that time the goods are sold and the value of them is converted into money. There is a risk that the sale will involve a loss, but it is very unlikely that the loss will be more than a small proportion of the total value. Thus a loan which covers only a proportion of the value is well secured.

This property of working capital is exactly what

the banks require for their short term loans, and it is naturally found that a great deal of the financing which is required for working capital is provided by means of short term loans.

Now it is clear that the volume of working capital which is required by business men is closely related to the volume of trade. A trader who believes that the demand for some commodity is likely to increase goes to his bank and obtains a credit to enable him to increase his stocks, and he then turns to the manufacturer and places a larger order. The manufacturer in his turn borrows money from his bank and increases his output. There is therefore a close relationship between trade activity and the volume of short term credit.

THE CONNECTION BETWEEN CREDIT AND SPENDING

Let us suppose then that the banker has agreed to provide the necessary credits and the manufacturer has taken on more workmen and has started to increase his output.

The first consequence is that the extra workmen go into the market and spend their wages, so that the credit provided by the banker for the manufacturer reappears as increased spending.

The second thing that happens is that the trader takes some of the increased output in the form of working capital, so that the credit provided by the banker to the trader absorbs goods from the market in this form.

Ultimately the goods reach the market. If the trader's prediction has been correct the goods are sold and manufacture continues on the higher scale. There is of course the difficulty that the additional spending power has taken effect before the extra supply of goods has become available for sale, but apart from this slight blemish the whole scheme is perfect. The granting of the credit has increased both spending and output, and employment has been found for so many extra men without any serious inconvenience to anyone.

HOW THE BANKER CAN EXPAND CREDIT

In theory at least the operation of expanding credit is a very simple one. All the banker has to do is to make advances to some of his customers, and these customers will in their turn pay the money to others who will add the amounts to their deposits. By a stroke of the pen the banker has thus increased both his advances (or assets) and his deposits (or liabilities).

A reduction in the bank rate can also be made use of at the same time, as the figure at which this rate of interest is fixed has considerable influence on traders and industrialists who are contemplating the expansion of their business. A reduction of the bank rate is in fact an invitation to prospective borrowers that the banks wish to lend.

There are in practice certain limitations to this power of expanding credit. A credit is only another name for a debt, and it must ultimately be repaid or repudiated, so that the banker has always to consider whether the real assets on which the edifice of credit is erected are adequate for the purpose. It may also happen that potential borrowers who are in a position to offer adequate security are yet unwilling to come forward owing to their inability to find any profitable use for the money.

Putting aside these considerations for the moment, however, it appears at first sight that the banks do possess the power of expanding credit, and that expanding credit not only enables traders and industrialists to produce more goods, but also gives to individual consumers the necessary spending power wherewith to purchase them.

A FINANCIAL UTOPIA

It is small wonder that the conclusion at which we have arrived should inspire budding economists with dreams of a financial Utopia in which there would exist as much work as each man may wish to do.

"For they argue thus. Money (meaning loans) is the life blood of industry. If money (in this sense) is available in sufficient quantity and on easy terms we shall have no difficulty in employing to the full the entire available supply of the factors of production. For the individual trader or manufacturer 'bank credit' means 'working capital'; a loan from his bank furnishes him with the means to pay wages, to buy materials and to carry stocks. If, therefore, sufficient bank credit was freely available, there need never be unemployment. Why then, he asks, if the banks can create credit, should they refuse any reasonable request for it? And why should they charge a fee for what costs them little or nothing? Our troubles seem to him to arise because the banks have monopolised this power of creating credit in order to enable them, by artificially restricting its supply, to charge a price for it and thus realise a profit. For why, if they possess this magical power, are they so stingy? Why should industrialists have less working capital than they desire, or be compelled to pay 5 per cent for it? There can be only one answer: the bankers, having a monopoly of magic, exercise their powers sparingly in order to raise the price. If bakers were a close corporation who could make bread from stones, it does not follow that they would reduce the price of the loaf to the cost of a quartern of stones. Where magic is at work, the public do not get the full benefit unless it is nationalised." (13)

What then is wrong with this attractive picture? Some reference has already been made to this matter in Chapter II, but I may add a further reply in the form of a parable.

Once upon a time there was a certain trader who dealt in top hats. He was a zealous man and anxious to expand his business, and he communed with himself as to how this might be done. And he said to himself, "I will start an advertising campaign, and I will sell five times as many top hats as I do now, and I will become rich."

And the trader went to his banker and said to him, "I am about to expand my trade, and I desire credits for the purpose." And the banker saw that the trader was a man of energy and deserving of support and he gave him his credit. And the trader went to the manufacturer and said to him, "I am about to expand my trade, can you supply me with more top hats?" And the manufacturer said to the trader, "You are a man after my own heart, I will supply you with as many top hats as you wish." And he also obtained credits from his banker.

And in due course the trader received his top hats and launched his advertising campaign, and sales increased and all appeared to be well. But the wives of the citizens said to themselves, "We require new bonnets and why should our men waste their money in top hats?" and they were angry.

And it came to pass that the demand for top hats fell off, and the trader's campaign was a frost, and he found himself in possession of many top hats which no one would buy. And the banker, hearing of these things, demanded the return of his credit, and the trader offered him top hats but was unable to return the money. And the banker was angry and made the trader a bankrupt, and for many months refused credits to those that asked for them.

And other traders came to the manufacturer and

demanded bonnets, and he set to work in haste to alter his factory to produce bonnets instead of top hats. And he was angry that his trouble should have been wasted, and that he should have lost money.

And the citizens demanded bonnets and could not be supplied with them and they were angry. And everyone was displeased.

And the moral is that it is no good producing commodities which the public will not buy. The problem which the business world has to solve is not how to produce more goods, which is easy, but how to produce the right kind of goods, which is difficult.

RESPONSIBILITY FOR THE VOLUME OF CREDIT

We may now return to the question as to whether the banker or the business man is to be held responsible for determining the volume of short term credits, and the short story which I have ventured to introduce into the previous section may help to illustrate their respective functions.

In making the first decision as to whether a credit is to be granted or not both parties are quite free to act or not as they deem best. Unless the banker believes that the credit position is sound he is not compelled to lend, and unless the trader believes that his operations will be profitable he is not compelled to borrow. It would appear then that both sides must be regarded as responsible for any decision which is ultimately arrived at.

As regards the ultimate outcome of the business for which a credit has been obtained the responsibility must rest I think almost entirely on the business man. It is his business to foresee the future course of the market, and it is on the correctness or otherwise of his prediction that success or failure ultimately depends.

In regard to the problem of stimulating the expansion of trade after a slump the position is very similar. The banker can assist matters by providing an ample supply of credit at low rates of interest, but he cannot compel his clients to make use of it. It is only when the trader and the manufacturer see a hope of making profits that the credits are actually created and the expansion of industry begins. "If people think that any business that they do is likely to involve them in loss they would evidently be fools to do it, even if the money needed was lent them for nothing." (14) Far from being the villain of the piece as is popularly believed, the banker's role appears to be one of quite minor importance. "Banking action necessarily follows, not leads, industry." (15)

In actual fact a serious slump in trade usually leads to a period of cheap credit, and, when this stage has been reached, recovery is evidently a problem for the business man and not for the banker.

THE PROPER USE OF SHORT TERM LOANS

The previous sections have dealt with what may be called the orthodox use of short term credit in connection with the requirements of trade. In recent years, however, a great deal of money has been lent by banks and others under quite different conditions.

Money is lent for example to industrial firms in the hope that the loans will be repaid in due course by the issue of shares to the public. Nominally the terms of the loan provide that it is repayable to the bank at short notice, but this form of arrangement is only a polite fiction. In actual fact the bank has made an industrial investment which for window dressing purposes it prefers to regard as a short term loan.

Again money is lent to farmers and the security takes the form of a mortgage on the farm and stock. Here again the bank has the nominal right of insisting on the repayment of the money, but in actual fact the bank has become a sleeping partner in a business which it cannot manage if the active partner becomes insolvent, and which in times of depression cannot be sold to anyone else.

Again money is often advanced on the security of stocks and shares, and is used by the borrower for the purposes of speculation. Thus a man who has £1,000 worth of securities can probably borrow £800 and reinvest this sum in further securities on the strength of which he can borrow more money, so that in the end he may own securities of the nominal value of £4,000 subject to a bank debt of £3,000. In the event of a slump in which the securities fall to half their original value, the borrower becomes bankrupt, and the bank loses £1,000.

It is clear then that the power of expanding credit is an instrument which must always be used with due regard to the character of the assets which are offered as security for the loans. Nor is it sufficient to label the advances "Liquid Assets." The important thing is not the label on the package but the actual nature of the contents.

CHAPTER IX

TRADE CYCLES

INSTABILITY

THERE is a type of weighing machine in common use in which the weight of an article placed in the scale pan is indicated by the movements of a pointer on a scale. When the article to be weighed is first placed on the pan forces are set up which tend to move the pointer towards its new position. But this is not the whole problem which has to be solved by the designer. The moving parts possess inertia and there is a tendency for the pointer to overshoot the mark and oscillate about the correct position, and the designer must arrange matters so that these oscillations are damped out as quickly as possible. The ideal machine is one which is "dead beat," that is to say it should move with as little delay as possible to its correct position and without any oscillations at all. An unstable machine which went on oscillating and refused to come to rest would evidently be of very little value.

It is now well established that the industrial machine shows definite signs of instability, and the volume of production, price levels and so on are subject to fluctuations of considerable magnitude. The more important questions which arise in relation to these fluctuations are:—

Firstly, how do trade fluctuations arise?

Secondly, are all fluctuations of similar type, or is it possible to recognise different types?

Thirdly, what determines the period of the fluctuation, that is to say the time which elapses between one boom (or slump) and the next?

Fourthly, is the economic structure stable or unstable? In other words, when a lack of adjustment arises from any cause, does the disturbance tend to increase or diminish?

Fifthly, if the economic structure is unstable, how does it come about that booms and slumps ever come to an end?

These questions must now be examined.

CYCLICAL DISTURBANCES

When we study physics, astronomy, electricity, mechanics and similar subjects we are accustomed to find cyclical disturbances having exact periods, and it is then possible to identify particular oscillations and relate them to particular causes. In economics on the other hand the material dealt with is of a different character, and the exact repetition of any particular form of disturbance is not to be expected.

Statistical investigations of trade cycles have suggested that particular periods can be recognised but they have not been identified with particular causes, and it is necessary therefore to deal with the problem in somewhat general terms.

Bearing in mind these necessary reservations, it is convenient to use some of the nomenclature which is commonly used in describing disturbances which are truly periodic. "The period" of a cycle for example is the time which elapses between one boom (or one slump) and the next.

A PRODUCTION CYCLE

We have already taken note of the general character of the problem which confronts the business man, and we have seen how it is determined by the consumer's constantly changing demands, and the delay which inevitably occurs between the realisation of the customer's requirements and the actual production of the required article. Predictions as to future needs can never be exact, and it is natural that times should occur when particular articles are either too scarce or over-abundant.

This line of thought suggests a purely hypothetical case which I have called a pure production cycle, and which may be described as follows.

Let it be assumed that consumption is constant, but that production is variable and not correctly adjusted to consumption.

Let us start our investigation at a moment when stocks of commodities are high but production is below consumption, so that stocks are diminishing, and let us call this period of trade depression or diminishing stocks the first phase. Since stocks cannot go on diminishing for ever it is obvious that some form of adjustment is inevitable.

In fact as soon as the trend of events has made itself clear, traders and manufacturers will realise that there is likely to be a shortage of commodities and steps will be taken to increase production. The first step is to increase the supply of raw materials. The raw materials then pass through various intermediate stages, and finally, after several months, the finished product becomes available to the consumer. We thus pass into the second phase, a period of increasing production, or what is commonly called a trade boom.

By the time that the increased production becomes effective, however, stocks will be seriously depleted, and the demand for further production will be insistent. Production will therefore continue to increase. Nor is it possible to call a halt when production has drawn level with consumption. The depleted stocks must be made good, and for this purpose abnormal production is essential.

We thus enter upon a third phase, a period which starts with depleted stocks of commodities and which is distinguished by the fact that production exceeds consumption, that is to say a period of great trade activity.

As soon as the tendency is clear manufacturers and traders will again take action and will take steps to reduce production. It does not pay to keep half-finished goods, however, and such goods will naturally be completed in order to avoid loss. A decision to reduce production is therefore subject to delays of the same type as those which are involved when production is to be expanded, and by the time that production is reduced stocks will have increased to an abnormally high figure.

The fourth and final phase, commonly known as the slump, is one in which production is falling, and this phase must evidently continue until the surplus stocks begin to diminish, that is to say until production falls below consumption. Only when these surplus stocks of commodities are falling do we return to our starting-point, a position in which stocks are high and production is below consumption.

The pure production cycle described above is probably a reasonably accurate description of what may occur in the case of a single industry if trade in general is fairly stable. The teaching of experience will obviously enable predictions to be made with increasing accuracy, and such disturbances will evidently tend to die out. In other words pure production cycles do not involve instability in the economic structure as a whole.

The period of the cycle is evidently determined by the time which elapses between the starting of manufacture and the completion of the finished article. If this time is assumed to be nine months for example, and is identified with the length of one phase of the cycle, then the whole period would be three years.

TRADE ACTIVITY AND SPENDING

The previous section dealt with fluctuations which might affect the position of a single industry. We now turn to factors which affect trade and industry as a whole.

In the first phase of a production cycle a moment is reached when increased production is decided on, and the immediate effect of this decision is that a number of workers, previously unemployed, are taken into employment. The wages paid to these workers represent increased spending power and this increased spending power will certainly be made use of.

It comes about therefore that a decision to increase production has the immediate effect of increasing consumption. This increases the gap already existing between production and consumption, a gap which is not filled until a much later stage when the new commodities actually reach the market.

Similarly when production is in excess of consumption a decision to curtail production reacts on spending and diminishes consumption and further aggravates the situation.

If the increased consumption and the increased output of commodities took place at the same time the position would probably be stable, but the time occupied in manufacture introduces what an engineer would call a difference in phase between the fluctuations of production and the fluctuations of consumption.

The situation is one with which electrical engineers are familiar, and they know that a difference in phase between a current and the motive force which produces it is a source of instability unless the motive force is subjected to some independent means of control. Unfortunately the methods which are adopted by electrical engineers for the control of electromotive forces do not appear to be applicable to the problems which confront their economic colleagues.

PRICE LEVELS

Returning once more to the first phase in the production cycle we note that the decision to increase production indicates an ever-increasing gap between production and consumption. There will be a shortage of commodities, buyers will be more numerous than sellers and market influences will drive up prices.

So far as the consumer is concerned the rise of prices will tend to counteract his increased spending power, but this effect is not the most important one.

A trader who in the normal course of events holds a certain stock of commodities will find that this stock has increased in value during the time it has been in his possession, and that he is making special profits over and above the normal return which he expects to get from his business. This stimulates trade, and everyone tries to get a share of the profits by buying something and selling it to someone else at a profit. And so long as prices go on rising the whole matter is so simple that failure is almost impossible. We are in fact in the midst of a trade boom.

The ease with which money can be made during a boom also affects the position in another way. Those who made money easily naturally spend it readily, and so easily made profits are quickly spent and consumption is further augmented.

Rising prices and the profits which arise therefrom furnish therefore a very strong stimulus to trade which serves to increase the instability of the whole structure.

We have thus reached a point in our argument which makes it possible to review the position which arises when trade is expanding, and which enables us to study the play of cause and effect.

The efforts of manufacturers to expand production involve increased employment and perhaps higher wages, and these mean increased spending, or an increased demand for commodities. The increased demand raises prices and increases profits, and thus stimulates the trader and manufacturer to further efforts. It would not in fact be very wide of the mark to say that the windfall profits made during a boom resemble the impulses which are given to the pendulum by the driving mechanism of a clock. They provide the energy which sustains the oscillations.

Expanding trade, increased demand, higher prices

and increased profits thus form a chain of cause and effect which leads to further expansion of trade, and so on. In other words expanding trade is cumulative in its effects, and the whole system suffers from inherent instability.

A brief reference must also be made to other factors which tend in the same direction.

CREDIT

Since the volume of working capital depends on the activity of trade, and since working capital provides much of a bank's most suitable assets, a trade slump naturally compels bankers to contract credit to keep pace with the reduction of assets.

Apart from this, however, a slump in trade reduces the value of any security which has been offered for a loan, and there will arise cases in which borrowers will decide to call in their loans. This means that bonds, shares, mortgages and so on will be thrown on the market, and the fall in prices will be still further accentuated. The larger the volume of credit (or debt) which has been created during the boom the more severe must be the slump before things can take a turn for the better. (16)

WAGES

When trade is good and wage-earners are pretty fully employed, there is a tendency for employers to pay higher wages in order to maintain production at its highest possible level. In times of depression on the other hand there is extensive unemployment and wages will tend to fall.

These changes in wages affect the spending power of the workers and tend to accentuate the severity of boom or slump as the case may be.

INVESTMENT

Factors which affect investment are discussed elsewhere, but there is an important link between production and investment which may conveniently be referred to here.

A brisk demand for commodities naturally leads to a demand for increased facilities for their production so that a high level of production means increased opportunities for investment. At the same time the construction of new factories provides employment, increases spending and generally stimulates activity in trade. Conversely, when trade is bad and production is low, the demand for new factories vanishes and unemployment is increased. It is to be expected therefore that there will be a certain degree of correlation between activity in trade and activity in investment, and it is a matter of general experience that such correlation is actually found to exist.

At the same time it is necessary, I think, to distinguish between two distinct types of fluctuation, involving two distinct types of trade depression, which may be referred to as trade slumps and investment slumps respectively. Nor must we allow the position to be obscured by the fact that a trade slump is usually associated with a certain falling off in investment, and an investment slump may synchronise with a slump in trade. The distinction between the two types of disturbance must be traced to a fundamental difference in the primary causes by which the slump has been caused, and must depend to a considerable extent on the soundness or otherwise of the investment position existing at the time.

If the capacity of the factories and other means of production is such that the total output can be absorbed by potential customers, or if the margin of productive capacity is only slight, then the position can be regarded as sound. The normal expansion of trade will give rise to fresh opportunities for investment, and the falling off in the supply of new investments will only be temporary.

On the other hand the existence of an excessive number of factories or other means of production may create a situation in which the actual and potential requirements of consumers can be adequately met, not only for the moment, but also for several years ahead, and this will be especially the case if investment has been in the direction of increasing the output of established industries rather than the creation of new ones. Under such conditions the falling off in the building of new factories and in the supply of new investments may last for a long time, and the slump will differ considerably in character from the trade slumps which have been discussed in this chapter. The general effect will be that the investment slump will be of longer duration than the other, and the depression created will be more acute.

THE INFLUENCE OF THE BANKS

The power of the banks to influence the volume of credit has already been referred to, and the question arises therefore as to the extent to which bankers can influence or control the fluctuations which have been described in the previous sections. There are clearly two types of situation in which such control would be desirable; firstly, it might be applied to the restriction of trade activity when it has become clear that production is outrunning consumption, and secondly, it might be applied to facilitating the expansion of trade after a slump.

In actual fact the banks do try to influence the position in the manner indicated, but experience shows that their powers in this direction are distinctly limited. During a boom the profits which can be made on buying and selling shares and commodities may considerably exceed the amount of interest which the trader or speculator has to pay to his bank, and a boom usually continues for some time after the banks have realised the danger, and in spite of any efforts which they may make to stop it.

Similarly, the period of stagnation which succeeds

a slump is not easily curtailed by any action which can be taken by the banks. Cheap credit is a normal feature of such conditions, and is obviously necessary in order to provide for the period of expansion which must follow in due course, but it is not in itself sufficient to ensure a return to prosperity. The expansion of trade and industry is a matter for business men rather than for bankers, and it is only when the business community begins to see its road clearly before it that trade and industry begin to revive.

Nor is it desirable that the process of recovery should be unduly hastened, for excessive haste can only lead to fresh over-production in particular directions, and can only serve to impair confidence and make matters worse. When trade and industry expand it is essential that they should expand in the right direction, and this desirable result is only attainable by a combination of the best efforts of the trader, the manufacturer and the investor. It is on the correctness or otherwise of their joint decisions that success or failure ultimately depends.

POSSIBLE IMPROVEMENTS IN THE SYSTEM

The value of business foresight in controlling and modifying the extent of trade fluctuations is sufficiently obvious, but it is not easy to suggest means by which this desirable quality may be encouraged.

There is, however, another field for improvement which seems worthy of consideration. In mechanical structures excessive oscillations are normally cured by making the structure stiffer. This causes the frequency of the oscillations to increase while their amplitude is diminished. There are other remedies which are applicable in special cases but they need not concern us here.

If this principle is applied to the problem of trade cycle and in particular to the phase of trade cycle when trade is contracting the following ideas suggest themselves:—

(i) Flexibility in wages is not desirable, and reductions of wages should be avoided if possible.

(ii) Flexibility in prices is not desirable, and industries should try to control output rather than leave individual firms to the fate of cut-throat competition.

(iii) The curtailment of normal spending is not desirable. Individuals should rather balance their family budgets by reduced savings.

(iv) In so far as it does not produce undesirable reactions unemployment pay would appear to be beneficial since it prevents the spending power of the wage-earners from disappearing altogether.

In regard to the last two suggestions I should perhaps explain that I have assumed that saving is still sufficient to provide for all proper requirements of trade and industry. If the slump has been severe this is normally the case.

REDUCTION OF WAGES

From what has been said in Chapter VI it is clear that reductions in rates of wages will increase the shareholder's profits (or reduce his losses), and this fact has led certain economists to advocate reductions of wages as a remedy for unemployment.

One obvious objection to the proposal is that it will certainly be resisted by the wage-earners themselves, and that attempts to enforce it will lead to strikes and other social and economic disturbances. But this is by no means the only objection.

An important point which must be noted is that a reduction of trade losses cannot be regarded as having the same significance as the attainment of that critical point at which losses change into profits. Unless reductions of wages are accompanied by other steps tending also to increase profits, the effect on profits may be inadequate and the general result may be without importance.

There are also other effects to be considered. The transfer of spending power from the wage-earner to the shareholder will probably lead to a greater volume of saving, and this result may be beneficial, or it may not. If credit is scarce and rates of interest are high, action calculated to increase the shareholder's profits at the expense of the bondholder may place a fresh obstacle in the way of recovery, and reductions of wages may be the lesser evil. On the other hand if credit is plentiful and rates of interest are low, action calculated to reduce the bondholder's portion would seem to be less open to objection than reductions of wages.

THE PROGRESS OF THE SLUMP

In the previous section reference has been made to various causes of instability, and it has been shown that certain factors act in such a way that a trade depression, once started, tends to become deeper. It is inevitable that this process should continue until these influences have spent their force. Abnormal stocks of materials must be absorbed, the credit structure must be reduced, production where excessive must be curtailed and so on.

As regards positive action to minimise the evil effects of a slump, experience seems to show that the mistakes of the past must be paid for, and that attempts to bolster up an unstable position are futile. The best that can be done is to liquidate the position as rapidly as possible.

There is, however, one important point which is deserving of attention. The later stages of a period of trade activity and the early stages of a slump are usually associated with a period of dear credit, and an abundant supply of cheap credit is one of the factors which is necessary for recovery. During the early stages of a slump therefore it is desirable that everyone should economise since cheap credit is one of the first conditions for the recovery of trade and industry.

THE PROCESS OF RECOVERY FROM A PERIOD OF TRADE DEPRESSION

In due course the liquidation of weak positions and the other factors already referred to cause a slowing down of the decline, and the slump merges into a phase of general depression and stagnation, and this transition is usually marked by the appearance of cheap credit together with a lack of suitable opportunities for making use of it.

In addition to cheap credit the process of recovery needs the assistance of a second factor, namely a condition of affairs in which the trader and industrialist can foresee profits. Of the factors which appear to be necessary for the purpose the following appear to be the most important.

Firstly, a slump reduces the opportunities for investment, and ultimately causes a fall in the rates of interest both for loans and for investments. Calculations as to whether an enterprise is profitable or not involve the interest on capital as an item of cost, and a fall in the rate of interest in itself reduces costs, thus making the enterprise more "profitable" in the economic sense even though the earnings available for the payment of dividends remain unchanged.

Secondly, liquidation wipes out many of the bondholder's rights, and thereby reduces the portion of the national dividend to which the bondholder is entitled.

Thirdly, there may be reductions in wages. In recent times changes in the rates of wages in Great Britain have not been great, but elsewhere there have been changes of considerable significance.

Fourthly, the fall in prices will lead to a curtailment of production. A boom in trade always involves over-production in certain directions, and recovery is impossible until production is reduced. The fall in prices which accompanies a slump must eventually compel the necessary fall in production. It is interesting to note in this connection that an unorganised industry is much more seriously affected by a slump than an industry which is protected by an effective monopoly. The monopolist can reduce production without reducing prices and without serious loss of profits, whereas an unorganised industry is compelled to go through the phase of falling prices and heavy losses before the necessary control of production becomes effective.

The question of the means which are available for assisting recovery will be dealt with in Chapter XX.

CHAPTER X

INVESTMENT

CHARACTERISTICS OF AN INVESTMENT

In the course of a few months raw materials pass through the various stages of manufacture and emerge as finished products and are sold to the consumers, so that the money which has been spent on them reappears as money again. But it is not so with investments.

Money which has been invested in factories and machinery has disappeared as such, and has reappeared in a new form in which value depends on earning power. The original owner may sell the factory to someone else, but, from the point of view of the community as a whole, the money which was originally spent has gone, and something of an entirely different kind has taken its place.

In this connection it may be well to mention that the word "investment" is often used in a wider sense than is here defined, that is to say a man who saves money and buys shares with it is said to "invest" his money. In the present essay the word "investment" is applied only to the original transaction in which money which has been saved is spent on such objects as the construction of a factory or the purchase of machinery.

DISTURBING FACTORS

In time of war the normal flow of investment is interrupted in order to provide the means for carrying on the war.

Again, if the national budget is not balanced, individual savings which should be available for investment will be dissipated in other directions.

Or again, if wage-earners and bondholders secure abnormal portions of the national dividend, the shareholders' profits will disappear and with them all incentive to business expansion.

Under any of these circumstances trade and industry will be impeded and will fail to pursue their natural course. In order to study the development of trade and industry under what may be called normal conditions it must be assumed that such disturbing factors are absent.

A SIMPLE CASE

A professional man who is earning a good income and who has more money than is necessary in order to satisfy his immediate needs will naturally desire to save some of his income in order to provide for his old age and for the various claims of his family.

The spending power which the individual possesses but does not desire to make use of for his immediate needs may be diverted to the construction of a factory, the earnings of which will ultimately return to the investor his original investment with interest.

The picture which is thus created in our minds serves to illustrate the fundamental relationship between saving and investment, but before the one can be identified with the other it is necessary to make allowance for certain necessary adjustments.

Thus it must be remembered that saving may be carried out by joint stock companies as well as by private individuals, and it must also be noted that money which is saved and available for investment may be hoarded or it may be diverted into the short term loan market to supply the need for working capital.

JOINT STOCK COMPANIES

Trade has always fluctuated between periods of activity and periods of depression, and a company which is carefully managed seldom distributes the whole of its profits in the shape of dividends. In good years a part of the earnings is set aside as a reserve and this money is usually invested in gilt-edged securities so that it can be easily realised in time of need.

In this manner joint stock companies become large investors in gilt-edged securities, and their method of handling their reserves is an important factor in the market for investments. The accumulation of reserves in this manner is of course a form of saving, and has precisely the same effects as saving by individuals. The difference lies in the motives which inspire the saving and the difference in policy which results therefrom. In the case of private individuals there appears to be quite definite evidence that saving is always in progress. It may vary in amount, but it never vanishes altogether. In the case of joint stock companies on the other hand there are periods when reserves are being sold instead of being added to, and this type of operation may be regarded as negative saving.

THE DEMAND FOR SHORT TERM LOANS

Through the medium of deposits the banks control a considerable volume of money which has been saved but which has not been invested by its original owner, and, in virtue of their position as guardians of this money, the banks exercise a powerful influence on the amount of money available for investment.

It has already been explained that the banker's liability to repay his depositors in cash causes him to view short term loans with a high degree of favour. When there exists a general feeling of lack of confidence and people are showing a tendency to hoard their money, the banker is often hard put to it to find sound and suitable means for utilising his money, and he is always on the lookout for fresh securities of what he regards as the most appropriate type. Expanding trade involves additional working capital, provides the banker with what he is seeking, and tends therefore to draw away funds which would otherwise be available for investment.

Again, firms of good standing who are in a sound

financial position may issue additional shares and finance their expanding trade by money obtained directly from the public. In either case the result is the same, expanding trade claims the use of money for its own purposes, and the amount of money which is available for investment proper is correspondingly diminished.

When trade is contracting on the other hand it might be expected that the reduction in working capital would release extra sums which would be available for investment, but the situation is generally complicated by other factors. Falling prices may give rise to business failures, and money may be lost in attempting to bolster up a scale of production which is not justified by the circumstances. Cheap credit does not usually appear therefore until a slump is well advanced.

Broadly speaking it may be said that the amount of money diverted to the short term loan market is not usually sufficient to affect the amount available for investment to any serious extent. It is only in times of rapidly expanding trade that this demand becomes important, and the factor must even then be regarded as a temporary one.

HOUSING

The business of constructing houses is a fairly extensive one, and on this account is not without importance. From the economic standpoint it has certain peculiarities which are deserving of notice.

Factories and machinery owe their value to their earning power. They are of little value in themselves but owe their value to the fact that they are used for producing something else. Houses on the other hand are of direct value to the user. For this reason the financing of house construction is accompanied by very little risk. New houses are always wanted in greater or less numbers and a falling off in demand is soon adjusted by reducing the supply.

Apart from this particular characteristic houses retain their value for long periods of time and may therefore be regarded in the light of investments.

The demand for new houses is no doubt affected by the general state of business, that is to say by the amount of spending by the community as a whole, but it must also be influenced to a very great extent by the rate of interest at which money is available for investment. The rate of interest at which money is available for construction is a large item in the rent, and a reduction in rents would certainly be expected to stimulate the demand for better houses.

WHO IS THE INVESTOR?

It is often said that the average shareholder knows little or nothing of the business in which his money is invested. A new enterprise may perhaps be financed in the first instance by the banks, and the shares may afterwards be introduced to the public through the medium of some issuing house whose business it is to arrange matters of that sort. The individual investor is no doubt influenced to some extent by the advice of his stockbroker and by the record of the house which has made the issue, but it is impossible to ignore the fact that the shareholder is the man who has the money and who has also the power of calling the tune if he wishes to exercise it.

In the case of commercial enterprises the issuing house is influenced by the views of manufacturers and by the opinions of technical experts, and it will be guided to a considerable extent by the manufacturer's previous record. The opinion of a man who has been successful in previous enterprises will naturally carry more weight than the opinion of one who has failed or who is lacking in practical experience. A serious responsibility rests therefore on those who hold such positions of authority.

Ultimately, however, the value of an investment is determined by its earning power, and the failure of one particular investment will tend to dissuade investors from putting any more money into ventures of a similar character. Default by a foreign government in the payment of interest or the failure of a commercial enterprise to earn dividends is a more potent influence than the advice of any stockbroker or the blandishments of any issuing house.

Be all this as it may someone must decide whether the money required for some particular enterprise is to be provided or not, and I shall call this person "the investor." I must leave it to each individual citizen to decide to what extent he or she is responsible for the serious indiscretions for which this ghostly personality must certainly be held responsible.

THE IMPORTANCE OF THE INVESTOR'S DECISIONS

If an investor puts his money into some enterprise which ultimately ends in failure, he loses his money, and he may well believe that the affair is nobody's business but his own. In actual fact however the loss of the investor's money is often the least serious consequence of a commercial failure on a large scale.

To establish a new industry does not merely involve the erection of a factory and the design of a quantity of machinery, it involves the training of a number of workers to whom the industry provides a means of livelihood. And it is the loss of employment which necessarily results from an industrial collapse which presents by far the most serious problem.

If the industry is well established and if its expansion has been gradual the difficulties which arise in finding employment for the displaced workers assume their most serious form. Many of the displaced workers may be too old to learn a new trade, and the question of providing adequate housing in some new locality may also be a serious matter.

Errors in directing the course of investment declare themselves more slowly and take longer to correct than errors in relation to production. A wise control of investment is therefore the more important of the two. At the same time it is unfortunately the more difficult.

THE INVESTOR'S DIFFICULTIES

The control of production in such a manner as to keep pace with consumption is the problem which faces the trader and the manufacturer in the ordinary course of their business. It requires that they should make predictions six, twelve or eighteen months ahead of the time when the commodities are to reach the consumer, and it is a problem which is hard enough to solve correctly.

The problem which faces the investor is an infinitely harder one. A factory probably takes a year or two to complete and the proper organisation of the staff required for a new industry may take several years. But the mere fact that the business has been started and is producing something at a profit is no evidence that the enterprise has been successful. It is not until it has been in successful operation for ten or fifteen years that it can be said to have yielded an adequate return for the labour which has been expended in its development.

If the investor is to carry out his duties in a satisfactory manner therefore, he must foresee the course of business ten, fifteen or twenty years ahead.

Is it to be wondered that he sometimes makes

mistakes, and that investment is sometimes directed into unproductive channels?

THE MAKING OF NEW ISSUES

In Great Britain new industrial enterprises have often been started by private individuals, and a number of enterprises are still promoted in this way, but in diminishing proportion. Private firms are gradually giving place to joint stock companies, and the introduction of new investments of this type is known as "company promoting" and is carried out by financial houses which specialise in that sort of business.

The results have not always been very happy. In the year 1928 the amount subscribed for capital issues in shares and debentures in 284 companies was £117 millions. On May 31, 1931, the total market value of these shares was only £66 millions, or slightly more than half the original figure. (17)

Many issuing houses have a high reputation and endeavour to deal honestly with their clients, but the system makes things all too easy for the dishonest company promoter whose sole idea is to make as much money as he can for himself without regard to his clients' interests.

It is not easy to suggest an effective remedy, but if someone would make a statistical analysis of the issues made by different firms and revise this publication annually, I think an important step would be taken in the right direction. The defaulting company promoter is usually responsible for a number of unsuccessful flotations before he finally ignores the rules and brings an inglorious career to a dramatic conclusion in the police courts.

In other countries the banks play a larger part in financing industry, and this arrangement no doubt reduces the risk of dishonest dealing, but it evidently leaves less scope for individual enterprise. When it comes to a question of deciding whether a particular type of business is sound or otherwise there is no reason to suppose that the banker is more likely to arrive at a correct decision than anyone else.

CHAPTER XI

THE BALANCE BETWEEN SAVING AND INVESTMENT

A BALANCE SHEET

When income is not spent on consumable commodities we say that it is saved, and there are three ways in which savings may be disposed of. They may be hoarded, they may be deposited at the bank or they may be invested.

As regards the money deposited at the bank, the banker in his turn will retain one part as cash, he will lend another part in some form of short term loan and he will invest the remainder.

The final result is that savings are either hoarded, lent on short term or invested. It is therefore possible to prepare a balance sheet in which savings appear on one side, and hoarding, short term loans and investment on the other.

Some economists define income, savings and investment in such a way that other items make their appearance in the balance sheet, but the expedient does not appear to be convenient and will not be adopted here.

As regards the item "investment" in this balance sheet it is important that the meaning in which the word is used should be clearly understood. When money is spent on the erection of a factory the transaction may be looked at from two points of view. On the one hand the sum involved represents the amount of the investor's savings, and on the other hand it represents the cost of the investment which has been created by the expenditure of the money. And since the two expressions are simply different names for the same thing they must obviously be equal.

It is important to note that neither the actual value of the factory nor the subsequent sale of the investment to some other person affects our balance sheet in any way. Such transactions merely represent changes of ownership. The aspect of the matter with which we are concerned is simply that a certain amount of money has been spent and that something different which we call an investment has taken its place.

THE NATURE OF THE PROBLEM

Let us now return to the consideration of our balance sheet.

On the one side we have:—

(i) The total amount of individual savings.
(ii) The amount saved by joint stock companies, which may be either positive or negative.

On the other side we have:—

(i) The increase in the hoards of private individuals in coin, notes or gold, which may be positive or negative. Bank deposits are not included.

(ii) The increase in the holdings of the banks in coin, notes or gold, which may be either positive or negative.
(iii) The increase in the amount of short term loans, which may be either positive or negative. This item is closely related to the amount of working capital required in trade.
(iv) The amount of new investment.

Now the essential thing about a balance sheet is that it must balance, and one naturally looks for the item which is sufficiently flexible to adjust itself to the changes which occur in the remainder. And here we come up against one of those problems which make the study of Economics so interesting. On the face of it there is no item which appears to possess the necessary flexibility. Let us take each in turn.

Individual saving is governed by motives which are obviously little affected by the supply of new investments, or by any of the other items on the balance sheet. Further, there is statistical evidence that it does not vary to the extent or in the manner which is required to affect the necessary adjustment.

The savings of joint stock companies are largely influenced by the condition of trade. When trade is good companies will add to their reserves, and when trade is bad reserves will be absorbed. The possibility that this item may be the key to the puzzle is discussed below.

Hoarding, either by individuals or by banks, is not normally of sufficient magnitude to provide the required adjustment. Money awaiting investment may be held up for a few months, but it is not likely to be held up for long. Hoarding except as a temporary factor must therefore be ruled out.

The demand for short term loans depends on whether trade is expanding or contracting. The amount involved is an important temporary influence but it is not sufficient to affect the balance sheet to a serious extent over long periods.

Finally we come to the question of new investment. Opportunities for investment are naturally related to the progress of science and invention, and the construction of the railway system, the increasing uses of electricity and the development of the motor industry naturally come to mind in this connection. But such developments have no apparent connection with the amount of saving.

THE ORTHODOX SOLUTION

The solution to this problem which has been put forward by many well-known economists is that savings in excess of investment are "wasted," and there is in fact statistical evidence that losses in trade and a deficiency of investments do often go hand in hand. (18)

Now the connection between excessive savings and trade losses is by no means obvious, and economists have therefore laboured to show how the connection arises. In these efforts expressions such as "forced saving," "automatic lacking" and so on make their appearance, and do not tend to make matters easier for the inexperienced wanderer in these fields of knowledge.

The criticism which I would venture to make of these efforts is that they have been directed towards an unattainable ideal in that they have attempted to discover a single formula to cover a number of distinct developments which are liable to arise in different ways and from different causes. This may be made clear by considering a certain number of examples.

SUCCESSFUL AND UNSUCCESSFUL INVESTMENTS

When a new industry is being developed and invention is active, it is usual to find that competing firms are rewarded with a very variable measure of success. Some particular industrialist may be better able to appreciate the possibilities of the situation and may make large profits, while his less fortunate rivals are making losses and gradually eliminating themselves from the field. Under such conditions those who have entrusted their savings to the successful manufacturer will obtain large returns, while less discriminating investors may lose their money. Viewed from a narrow standpoint the savings of the latter have been wasted. From a larger point of view, however, they may be regarded as casualties on the road of progress, and we may take the view that what really matters is the net volume of expenditure and the net result which has been produced.

Perhaps the chief importance of this example lies in the way in which it emphasises the difficulty of drawing any precise line between money which has been "invested" and money which has been "wasted."

UNSOUND INVESTMENT

As a variation on the previous theme there are cases in which money is invested in enterprises which existing knowledge and a reasonable judgement should have condemned as unsound. For some time everything may go well. There may even be a little boom and the enterprise may enjoy a temporary prosperity. Sooner or later however comes the day of reckoning, the enterprise collapses, and the investor realises that he has lost his money.

In such circumstances his savings have been truly wasted.

PERIODS OF TRADE DEPRESSION

During periods of trade depression two things will probably occur simultaneously. Manufacturers will find themselves losing money and will be compelled to realise some of their reserves, and at the same time opportunities for new investment will be reduced. The money which is saved by individuals will in fact be employed in two different ways. A part will provide for the reduced volume of new investment and the remainder will serve to cancel the "negative saving" of the manufacturers and traders.

Now this condition of affairs can be interpreted in two ways. We may adopt the attitude that the community would have been no worse off if the manufacturer had been unable to find a purchaser for his "reserves," and in that case we may argue that the investor's savings have been wasted.

On the other hand we may consider that the manufacturer has benefited through realising his reserves and that the investor has helped him round a nasty corner. The reader must be left to decide which view makes most appeal to him.

In this case the disparity between the volume of savings and the corresponding opportunities for investment is obviously accompanied by a loss of profits, but it is by no means clear that we are justified in regarding the former as the cause and the latter as the effect.

SPECULATION

There is yet another factor affecting the balance between saving and investment which may conveniently be referred to here, and that is speculation in stocks and shares.

In a general way it is evident that the buying and selling of stocks and shares, and the prices at which they are bought and sold, have no direct effect on our balance sheet. The transactions merely represent a change of ownership, and do not affect either the total volume of investment or the total volume of money. The importance of the buying and selling of shares does not in fact lie in this direction but is due to the indirect influence which such operations exercise on the actions of individuals and the consequent volume of spending.

The nature of the effect may be made clear by means of an example. Let us suppose that an investor, Mr. X, is concerned about the unsettled state of the markets, and that he decides to sell certain shares and place the money on deposit in his bank. The shares are bought by a speculator, Mr. Y, who holds them for a time, and then sells them at a profit to a business man, Mr. Z, who has been saving money and wishes to invest it. After a time the boom collapses and Mr. Z takes fright and sells the shares back to Mr. X at the price at which the latter originally sold them.

Now the crux of the whole matter is the attitude adopted by the various actors in the drama towards the events which I have described, and the way in which the buying and selling of shares affects their actions in other directions. If the operations were regarded in each case as increases or decreases of capital, the transactions would be simply changes of ownership and would have no other significance. It is unlikely, however, that Mr. Y, the successful speculator, will regard his profits in that light. He will regard them as income and will proceed to spend them.

From the point of view of the community at large, therefore, Mr. Z's savings have simply gone to support Mr. Y, a person who has rendered no service in return for them. The total amount of the national savings has been reduced by the amount gained and spent by the speculators, and it may once more be said that the savings have been wasted.

STIMULATING PRODUCTION

It is well known that an excess of savings seeking opportunities for investment tends to cheapen credit and stimulate production. If the tendency is not checked in time over-production ensues, and is followed in due course by a slump. These temporary fluctuations have already been discussed.

THE RATE OF INTEREST

The previous sections have dealt with what may be called special cases. There still remains the question as to what happens when trade is normal and the investor is wise enough to avoid the pitfalls of unsound investment. If savings still tend to outrun investment, what then?

To solve this problem it is necessary to turn to the principles of the market place. The commodity which is being offered for sale is money for investment and the price is the rate of interest. If therefore the supply exceeds the demand, the price, that is the rate of interest, should fall.

Now if the rate of interest does fall the opportunities for investment should be increased, and this increase should restore the balance between saving and investment.

Housing provides a good example of a type of investment which is likely to increase in volume as the rate of interest falls. Interest on the first cost of a house is the largest item in the rent. If the rate of interest is reduced everybody can afford a better class of house than he occupies at present and the building of houses may be expected to increase.

We are accustomed to think of housing in relation to a rate of interest of 5 or 6 per cent. If we could imagine housing financed on a 2 per cent or even a 3 per cent basis, we should realise that the whole situation would be profoundly modified.

I suggest therefore that opportunities for investment should eventually adjust themselves to the amount of saving through variations in the rate of interest, and that the volume of investment is in fact the most flexible item in the balance sheet. Savings are wasted if the investor shows lack of judgement and employs his money unwisely, but not otherwise.

THE LAST RESORT

There is yet one further possibility. Suppose that the rate of interest is very low, and that all suitable opportunities for investment both at home and abroad have been exhausted, what will happen then?

In this extreme case there is nothing for the investor to do but buy gold and hoard it. Or what comes to the same thing he may deposit his money in the bank, and the bank may be compelled to buy gold as the only possible means of disposing of the money. Something of this sort seems to have been taking place in France in recent years. (19)

CHAPTER XII

FOREIGN INVESTMENT

SOUND AND UNSOUND INVESTMENTS

FROM the creditor's point of view a satisfactory borrower should have two qualifications: he should have the necessary means to repay, and he should have the will to settle his debts justly and honourably as they fall due.

In considering the soundness or otherwise of foreign investments questions are involved which do not enter into the ordinary relationships between private individuals, but the two main factors are essentially the same. The debtor country must be actuated by a desire to repay, and there must at the same time be some practicable and accepted method by means of which repayment can be effected.

TWO TYPES OF INVESTMENT

Great Britain has been one of the pioneers in the business of foreign investment and one of its most successful exponents.

The urge to invest money abroad arose in the first instance from a desire to secure a supply of food and other raw materials which were necessary for the welfare of her industrial population. In this manner Great Britain has helped to finance the growing of wheat, cotton, tea, coffee, rubber and many other commodities.

The motive which inspired these efforts in itself led to investment upon sound lines. The enterprises that have been developed have been of great value to both debtor and creditor countries, and the payment of interest on the invested capital has in fact represented the capitalist's share of the total output. On the assumption that the creditor country does not itself produce the commodity in question, payment of interest can always be made by handing over a proportion of the commodity which is produced. The means of settlement is thus automatically available, and such investments may be called class A investments.

Industrial investments fall into a different category. Under modern conditions an industrial country can always supply from its own factories its own requirements of manufactured commodities, and there is a general tendency to exclude foreign industrial products by means of tariffs, so as to maintain home employment.

If therefore an industrial country lends money abroad, and if this money is used for building foreign factories designed for the production of commodities which the lending country itself produces, then payment of interest by means of the enterprise itself is no longer acceptable. Such investments may be called class B investments.

To put a more definite case. The United States

of America is a large producer of motor-cars. If money lent by the citizens of the United States or deposited by them in their banks is used for erecting motor-car factories in Germany, neither the loan itself nor the interest on it can be paid in motor-cars. Great Britain for a long time endeavoured to resist the idea that industrial imports are injurious to her home industries, but she has ultimately been compelled to capitulate, and it must now be accepted as a general principle that industrial countries will resist the importation of any articles which are capable of being manufactured at home without serious difficulty.

The question therefore arises, if payment in manufactured commodities is not admissible, are any other means available?

THE MEANS OF REPAYMENT

The repayment of international debts can be effected by five different methods, and I believe five only:—

(i) By cancelling debts due from the lender to the borrower.
(ii) By payment in commodities or services.
(iii) By payment in gold, silver or other valuables.
(iv) By promises of one kind or another.
(v) By political concessions.

I have excluded from this list the transfer of investments since such transactions only mean exchanging one form of promise for another.

The first method needs no comment: our problem really begins when this means of settlement has been exhausted.

The last-named method is only applicable in special cases, and I do not propose to discuss it.

There remain then three methods only—goods, gold and promises.

As regards gold the volume of debt which can be settled by this means is limited, and as regards promises these only remain acceptable while there is a hope of ultimate repayment. Both gold and promises are therefore temporary expedients. Sooner or later international obligations must be paid for in commodities or services, or they must be repudiated.

It becomes clear therefore that what have been called above class A investments are very much sounder than those which have been called class B. The latter type of investment may be charitable or it may be magnificent, but it is not sound business.

THE EVIL INFLUENCE OF THE GOLD STANDARD

Most international debts are payable in gold and the tendency for gold to rise in value is referred to elsewhere in this essay.

It might appear at first sight that this tendency would be to the advantage of the lender, but experience tends to show that it is not in fact to the ultimate advantage of either party to the transaction. The automatic increase in the real value of the creditor's claim which is due to the rise in the value of money increases the borrower's difficulties and decreases both his willingness and his ability to pay. It is the same type of problem which arises in connection with a country's internal debt to its bondholders. Sooner or later some crisis arises, the burden of the debt becomes intolerable, and the debt is repudiated either in whole or in part.

THE SECURITY OF FOREIGN INVESTMENTS

When two individuals belong to the same state the creditor can sue the debtor in the law courts and the debtor if he is solvent can be compelled to pay.

It is about half a century since Egypt became an international debtor to various countries in Europe. The bondholders were in that case sufficiently powerful to secure the military occupation of the country, and the consequent reorganisation of the whole administration not only secured the bondholder's interest on his investments but proved to be of lasting benefit to the Egyptians themselves.

The case of Egypt was obviously an exceptional one, and it is seldom possible for a creditor country to employ such methods for the collection of debts. A great deal has to depend on the debtor's national sense of honesty, and when this proves to be unequal to the strain lenders may bring some pressure to bear by refusing further supplies.

These considerations and the general result of

experience go to show that foreign investments are generally less secure than home investments, and that they require special caution on the part of the investor.

THE WILL TO REPAY

The will to repay being a matter of special significance in relation to foreign debts, it is important to notice that this force is likely to weaken with lapse of time.

A country may grant a monopoly to a foreign country in order to create some enterprise of public utility, or the government may borrow money abroad for the construction of railways or the erection of public buildings. So long as these developments are fresh in the minds of the borrowers the lender is looked upon as a public benefactor.

National memories in such matters are short, however, and in time the debtor's attitude undergoes a change. The existence of foreign monopolies is regarded as oppressive, and the payment of interest on foreign loans is regarded as a foreign tax not to be tolerated by an independent and self-respecting people. The benefits which the foreign loans conferred gradually sink into oblivion. It is well that lenders should realise these facts and that they should take into account the normal characteristics of human nature.

I cannot help thinking that it would be wiser to curtail the duration of foreign loans and foreign monopolies. If investors would regard a 6 per cent payment of interest as 4 per cent interest and 2 per cent sinking fund, they would I think save themselves from a great deal of anxiety and the world in general from a great deal of confusion.

DISHONEST BORROWERS

In the previous sections I have made the tacit assumption that the country which incurs the debts does so with the honest intention of repayment in due course.

When a country which is in need of money finds itself surrounded by lenders each with surplus cash and each more anxious than the other to provide the accommodation required, the temptation to rash and ill-considered borrowing is naturally very strong. In the period 1925 to 1930 the competition between lenders was unusually keen and led to a great deal of slackness and dishonesty on the part of the borrowers. Loans were obtained for the declared purpose of financing roads and railways and were spent on armaments, or money was squandered on projects which could never be of any real utility. (20)

The great difficulty about all this business is that the people who negotiate the loans make money out of the transaction, whereas both the debtor nation and the creditors are ultimately the losers.

THE DIFFERENCE BETWEEN HOME AND FOREIGN INVESTMENT

When a particular investment is under consideration the investor naturally endeavours to estimate the future prospects of the enterprise in which he proposes to invest his money. He looks at the result already obtained by the firm, studies the previous record of the management, and estimates the future market prospects for the products of the enterprise.

In considering the possibilities of investment in a foreign country the prudent investor must still bear all these matters in mind, but he must also examine another factor which has no counterpart in regard to home investment, and that is the trade balance.

If the imports are approximately equal to the exports, visible and invisible, both in his own country and in the country in which he proposes to invest, then all is well. Further, if the enterprise in which he is interested is designed to produce something which his own country is willing and anxious to import, or if it is possible to foresee some equivalent arrangement involving other countries, then the enterprise is sound and does not contain in itself the seeds of its own destruction.

On the other hand, if his own country has a balance of exports and the borrowing country a balance of imports, or if the product of his enterprise is unlikely to create a flow of trade from the foreign country towards his own, the investor should beware.

Instead of receiving back his money with interest he will probably be rewarded in due course with tales relating to difficulties in exchange and matters of that sort.

Sound foreign investment must take all these matters into consideration. As far back as 1925 the American investor was warned, "As matters stand, you can only collect your European war debts by reinvesting the proceeds in first-class European securities. As time goes on, the return on your European war debts and first-class securities will have to be reinvested in second-class securities, and then in third-, fourth-, and fifth-class securities, until finally the investments that you will be driven to hold go bust." (21)

The remark, which was made in regard to war debts, is of course equally true in regard to commercial debts, or debts of any kind.

CHAPTER XIII

THE TRADE BALANCE

IMPORTS AND EXPORTS

In early days, when trade was carried on by travelling merchants, each individual merchant took with him certain goods which he desired to sell, and in the course of his travels these goods were bartered for others with which he ultimately returned. Under such conditions of trade it is evident that there exists always an automatic balance between imports and exports.

Under modern conditions the business of importing and exporting is carried on by different people acting independently, and a balance between imports and exports must be secured by less direct methods.

The need for an approximate balance is generally admitted, and is I think sufficiently obvious. A country which exports too much is giving away its wealth without any adequate return, and a country which exports too little is living on the charity of its neighbours, and laying up for itself a time of trouble when its credit becomes exhausted. The need for adjusting one's expenditure to fit one's income is in fact even more necessary in the case of nations than it is in the case of private individuals.

VARIOUS ITEMS

The items which go to make up the complete account between any two nations may be divided into three groups, that is to say:—

(i) Goods and services.
(ii) Gold.
(iii) Foreign investments and foreign short term loans.

In addition to actual commodities the first group includes services such as tourist traffic and shipping, often referred to as invisible imports or exports as the case may be. Thus an English tourist in France is carried by the French railways and receives food and lodging at French hotels, so that the transactions have the same effect as if French goods were imported into England. Similarly, if French goods are taken to America in British ships the American consumer is receiving commodities whose cost is partly due to the services of the British shipping industry.

The group should also include interest on foreign investments, which can properly be regarded as a delayed payment for past services. To the debtor country the obligation to pay interest is an invisible import.

The total of all items which come under the heading of goods and services is the total volume of imports or exports as the case may be, and the difference between the two figures is the balance of trade. It is unfortunately a common custom to speak about an excess of exports as "a favourable trade balance" and an excess of imports as "an adverse trade balance," which naturally creates the impression that an excess of exports is more desirable than an excess of imports. In actual fact the former leads to an artificial stimulation of trade followed by a slump and serious unemployment, while the latter leads to insolvency. Unless we regard the matter from the point of view that it is more blessed to give than to receive, it is hard to see that one condition is more favourable than the other.

The exact determination of the total volume of imports and exports of goods and services is not an easy matter, and economists have devoted considerable attention to the statistical problems involved. The answer becomes known eventually with a moderate degree of accuracy, but only after a certain period of time. It is therefore easier to criticise the course of events than to exercise any effective control.

BALANCING THE ACCOUNT

The complete account, in which items belonging to all three groups are included, is made up of a vast number of separate transactions each of which is self-balancing, that is to say it includes on the one side goods and services and on the other side the gold or promises to pay which have been exchanged for them. It is therefore evident that the total account must balance, and that the trade balance which on the one hand is the balance of goods and services must be equal on the other hand to the value of gold and promises which have been used to pay for them. It is part of the orthodox theory of Economics that any undesirable excess of either imports or exports will eventually correct itself, and it is necessary therefore to enquire how this automatic balance is supposed to be brought about.

GOLD AND PRICES: ELEMENTARY THEORY

If gold, or something equally tangible, is the only accepted form of currency, both national and international, the required balance between imports and exports may be expected to establish itself automatically. A flow of commodities in one direction will involve a flow of gold in the opposite direction, and a country which is exporting too much will find itself with a surplus of gold. In accordance with the principle of the market place, the value of gold will fall, and the prices of commodities will rise. This rise in the prices of commodities will probably be reflected in the rate of wages, which will tend to rise also, and the rise in prices will thus be accentuated.

While this is going on in a country which has been exporting too much, the opposite effect is taking place in a country which is exporting too little, and the prices of commodities in the latter country will fall.

These changes in prices will evidently tend to reduce exports from the first country and increase exports from the second, and the lack of balance between imports and exports will thus be corrected. (22)

GOLD AND PRICES: MODIFIED THEORY

In the more highly developed countries gold is no longer used as currency, and the volume of money is not therefore the most important factor in determining prices. The result described in the previous section is still possible, but the mechanism by means of which the result is supposed to be brought about is different.

In a country equipped with a modern banking system it is not the volume of money which affects the price level, but the volume of credit, and the link between the volume of gold and the price level is provided by the policy of the banks. It is an established principle that a loss of gold should involve a restriction of credit, and *vice versa*, and the restriction of credit gives rise in its turn to a reduction of spending power. It is this reduced spending power which tends to produce a fall in prices. At the same time the restriction of credit and the reduction of employment also tend to lower wages. The ultimate result is therefore the same as if gold were the only form of currency.

FREE EXCHANGE

When a country is off gold the value of its currency in terms of gold or any foreign currency varies with supply and demand, and there is an immediate and direct connection between the trade balance and the price level. An excess of exports causes an immediate fall in the prices offered for exportable commodities, and *vice versa.*

What it really amounts to is that foreign trade becomes a question of barter, and currency hardly enters into the transactions at all.

The arrangement is a source of much inconvenience to traders, but it avoids the troubles which are necessarily involved in the use of an international currency.

LIMITATIONS OF THESE THEORIES

The elementary theory of automatic control makes the assumption that all payments, both internal and external, are settled in cash.

The modified theory assumes that internal payments may be made in paper, but that the balance of international payments is ultimately adjusted in gold.

The system of free exchange is a return to the time-honoured system of barter and obviously leads to an exact balance between imports and exports.

All these theories make the same assumption,

however; they assume that goods and services are paid for either in goods and services or else in gold. As soon as the transactions are run on a credit basis, however, instead of in cash, the automatic control ceases to be positive and definite as postulated in the above theories, and becomes flexible.

Let us consider then how this flexibility arises.

THE PRINCIPLE OF ARCHIMEDES

The relationship between the real trade balance, which is the difference between the imports and exports of goods and services on the one hand, and the flow of gold, investment and short term lending on the other, may conveniently be illustrated by means of a mechanical analogy.

The mechanical principle involved was expressed by Archimedes in the well-known saying that if he were given a fulcrum he could move the earth, and Newton expressed the same idea by saying that action and reaction are equal and opposite. The essential point is that it is never possible to apply an absolute force to any object; all that can be done is to set up a force between the object which we desire to move, which we call the load, and some other less mobile object, which we call the fulcrum. If the inertia of the fulcrum proves to be inadequate, our efforts will be largely expended in directions which are neither necessary nor desirable.

The application of this principle to the question of the trade balance is as follows. The real trade balance, that is to say the flow of commodities and services, represents the load, and the combination of foreign investment and foreign lending represents the fulcrum. So long as the fulcrum yields, the load will not move; that is to say so long as the lender is complacent the flow of commodities will continue. But so soon as the lender becomes anxious about the position and stiffens his attitude, the automatic control becomes effective; the irresistible force of circumstances compels the trade balance to return to zero quite irrespective of the inconvenient consequences which may be involved in the operation, and regardless also of special conditions which may make a certain lack of balance desirable in the common interest.

INVESTMENT IN NEW COUNTRIES

When a country possesses large but undeveloped sources of wealth it may be opened up with the help of foreign capital, and the new industries thus established may give rise to an export trade by means of which the original investment may be repaid.

In the early stages of such development there will be an excess of imports which will be paid for by means of the money lent by the foreign investor. At a later period the expansion of the new industries will give rise to an export balance which is accepted by the creditor country in payment of interest and sinking fund on the loans which have been made.

In many cases the payment of interest and sinking fund in connection with former loans proceeds at the same time as new investment in fresh enterprises, and the amount carried into the national balance sheet becomes the difference between these two sets of items.

The question as to whether particular foreign investments are sound or otherwise was discussed in the previous chapter, and on this matter of the soundness of the investments turns the further question as to whether a lack of balance between imports and exports is justified or not.

THE NEED FOR FLEXIBILITY IN THE TRADE BALANCE

Many products have a seasonal character, and particular countries may be subject to temporary setbacks owing to crop failures or similar causes, and it is evidently desirable that the international financial system should possess sufficient flexibility to smooth out these disturbances.

Movements of gold lead to a certain degree of flexibility in the trade balance, but the amount is strictly controlled by the policy of the banks, and there is an obvious limit depending on the amount of gold which is available for transfer.

Foreign investment, when carried out on sound lines, should not be of very large volume nor should it vary greatly from year to year.

The flexibility of the trade balance, which has

been a conspicuous feature of the situation since the war, may therefore be attributed in large measure to short term foreign lending, or to the transfer of bank deposits which for our present purpose may conveniently be regarded as a form of short term lending.

The nature of the problem of controlling this flexibility may be illustrated by comparing it to the problem of designing the springs of a motor-car. If the springs are made too stiff the passengers are jolted about as the car passes over the minor irregularities of the road surface, and we say that the springing is inadequate. On the other hand if the springs are not stiff enough, the body of the car may be brought up with a bump against the axle, or the car may sway dangerously when taking corners, or it may even upset.

There is evidence that the international financial system has been suffering from too much flexibility, and the severity of the present crisis is to be attributed, at least in part, to this defect. To put the matter quite bluntly, the flexibility of foreign lending has helped to upset the financial apple cart. However that is another story to which I hope to return in due course.

The theoretical position is that a certain amount of flexibility is desirable in order to alleviate the position of particular countries in times of abnormal difficulty. On the other hand excessive flexibility is extremely objectionable since it prolongs and accentuates any lack of balance, instead of allowing free play to economic forces, which, if left unhindered, would bring about the inevitable adjustment at the earliest possible moment.

WHY A LACK OF ADJUSTMENT TENDS TO INCREASE RATHER THAN TO DIMINISH

Except in so far as it pays in gold, a country which is importing more than it exports is evidently incurring debts equivalent in amount to the lack of balance in goods and services.

It has already been mentioned that interest on borrowed money must be regarded as an invisible import, and the effect of such obligations is to upset the trade balance still further. The lack of adjustment is cumulative, and tends to increase at an ever-accelerating rate.

As in so many other cases, it is found that the correction of the lack of balance involves some disturbance to trade and industry, but it is also clear that the longer the evil day is postponed, the greater must be the reaction when the time comes to face the inevitable.

CHAPTER XIV

TARIFFS AND SUBSIDIES

GENERAL CONSIDERATIONS

WITH tariffs which are imposed purely for revenue purposes we are not concerned here; the types of tariff which it is necessary for us to consider are those which are imposed with the special object of reducing imports and thus fostering and encouraging home industries.

Nor are we concerned with the more general arguments which are brought forward in support of tariffs or otherwise. Advantages of a political or military character, disadvantages such as the encouragement of monopolies, and so on are of great practical importance, but are beyond the scope of our present enquiry.

Even with this limitation, however, there remain certain considerations of very great importance to the prosperity of trade and industry.

TARIFFS AND THE TRADE BALANCE

Assuming that a protective tariff is effective, the immediate result of its introduction is to reduce imports, and the trade balance is affected accordingly.

In the case of a country which is importing too much, the introduction of protective tariffs tends to correct the adverse balance of trade, and enables a correct balance to be reached more quickly than would otherwise be possible, it being understood of course that a "correct balance" does not necessarily mean a zero balance; there may be adequate justification either for an excess of imports or for an excess of exports. Since the disturbance caused in correcting any lack of adjustment is only increased by delay, the introduction of tariffs under such conditions must be regarded as beneficial.

In other cases, that is to say when a country's trade balance is more or less correct, or when there is an excess of exports, the introduction of tariffs evidently upsets the existing balance or increases the lack of balance as the case may be; and, since any lack of adjustment is ultimately likely to set up forces which will force a balance, it is evident that the reduction of imports will ultimately lead to an equivalent reduction of exports. Like the village showman whose clients only have a limited amount of money to spend, the gains on the swings will be offset by losses on the roundabouts.

This aspect of the tariff question is all the more important because it often appears to be completely overlooked when tariff problems are under discussion. It may well be that the introduction of tariffs stimulates trade and industry, but, if that is the case, the stimulus is certainly a temporary one. The ultimate effect on employment is simply to divert trade from one industry to another; home industries expand and export industries contract to an equivalent extent.

Whether the ultimate effect of the change is beneficial or otherwise must necessarily be decided on its merits in each particular case.

SUBSIDIES

A shipping subsidy, if it is effective in expanding the mercantile marine of the country concerned, decreases the invisible imports and increases the invisible exports, so that, so far as the trade balance is concerned, subsidies have the same effect as tariffs.

EFFECTS OF TARIFFS AND SUBSIDIES ON THE MEANS OF PRODUCTION

The expansion of imports and the corresponding contraction of exports may be regarded as the primary effects of tariffs and subsidies. There is also a secondary effect, however, of no less importance.

The establishment of a home industry in any country which has hitherto satisfied its needs by importing evidently involves the suppression of a corresponding amount of industry in the country which has previously furnished these supplies; so that the change involves the duplication of the means of production and temporarily stimulates those industries which cater for the erection of factories and work of a similar character. Also the reduction of imports probably involves an equivalent reduction in exports and corresponding reactions in the other trades concerned.

The secondary effect produced by the introduction of tariffs, therefore, is an increase in the means of production, and it is to this secondary effect that most of the evil consequences of tariff barriers may be attributed.

Attention must also be directed to another important aspect of this question. The primary effects of tariffs and subsidies are reversible, that is to say the removal of a tariff would probably enable trade to return to its original channels. The secondary effect however is not reversible; once the means of production have been artificially expanded beyond the legitimate needs of the situation, the damage done is irrevocable. No subsequent reversal of the mistaken policies of the past can render useful the surplus ships and factories, or absorb the wage-earners who have been trained in unwanted occupations; the trouble is one which only time can cure.

CHAPTER XV

WAR FINANCE

INTRODUCTION

THE financial problems which present themselves in time of war are necessarily different from those which arise in time of peace, and a criticism of war-time finance forms no part of the scheme of the present essay. It is worth while giving a brief outline of financial events during the Great War, however, as it furnishes some instructive illustrations of the economic principles which have already been discussed. (23)

In the course of the narrative it will appear that workers were bluffed by the lure of high wages which actually enabled them to buy less, and that investors were bluffed into lending money which in the nature of things could never be repaid, but it must not be supposed that the governments in power were alive to the consequences of their own actions. In telling the story I have taken full advantage of recent developments in economic theory, and it is not to be assumed that this knowledge was available to the actors when the great drama was actually being played.

THE WAR PERIOD

In discussing war finance there are two distinct periods to be considered—the war period itself and the period of adjustment which immediately followed it.

During the war the aim of each belligerent was to secure the greatest possible output of munitions, and this consideration involved two important changes in the organisation of industry.

In the first place it was necessary to secure the greatest possible number of workers so that production might be increased in spite of the transfer of men from the workshop to the firing line. In times of peace there are many people who are suitable for employment in industry but who, for various reasons, are not so employed, and these people had to be absorbed. Further they had to be paid.

In the second place ordinary consumption had to be reduced so that the number of workers not employed on munitions should be as low as possible. Food and clothing for the civilian population were still needed, but anything over and above this had to be severely restricted. In other words it was necessary for everyone to economise.

Now economising, or saving, takes place quite naturally among the well-to-do even in peacetime. In war-time the manufacture of luxuries can be stopped, and extravagance of any sort is pretty well prevented by the force of public opinion, so that the well-to-do cannot help saving. With the wage-earners it is different, for they never have much more than the bare necessities of life. To have given them increased purchasing power would inevitably have meant that their consumption of commodities would have increased instead of diminishing.

The financial problem which resulted from this condition of affairs is therefore clear. It was necessary to employ more labour and at the same time to give this increased labour force less spending power. Theoretically perhaps wages and prices might have kept at the same level and the necessary funds might have been raised by taxing wages, but no government had the courage (or perhaps the power) to adopt this expedient.

In actual fact governments did not tax wages, but adopted almost unconsciously a policy which produced a similar effect. Under pressure from the wage-earners wages were allowed to rise, and at the same time prices were allowed to rise still faster. Therefore the wage-earners were kept contented although their spending power was reduced. At the same time the claims of existing bondholders were heavily reduced by the rise in prices.

The net result was that spending power was reduced all round, and thus the primary need of the situation was met. But the solution of the problem was still incomplete, for the spending power which was withdrawn from the community in general was not in the hands of the government. In accordance with the principles already explained in Chapter VI, the reduced shares of the wage-earner and the bondholder pass automatically into the hands of the trader and industrialist. In other words the spending power of which others had been deprived was poured into the lap of the profiteer, and it was then necessary for the government to decide how to take this spending power away from the profiteer and make it available for war expenditure. Two methods were available, taxes and loans.

Theoretically the whole of the money might have been taken in the form of taxes, and in that case there would have been no war debt and the post-war problem of adjustment would not have arisen. Taxes are unpopular, however, and in actual fact no government did attempt to solve the problem on these lines. In most of the belligerent countries very little of the money required was raised in the form of taxation and the bulk was obtained in the form of loans. In Great Britain on the other hand the sense of financial rectitude was stronger, and a fair proportion of the money was raised by means of special taxation.

In all cases the loans raised furnish an example of the balance between savings and investment. Having decided that the money required to pay for the war was to be regarded as an investment, it was necessary that someone should possess the means and the incentive to carry out the corresponding saving. Thus the profiteers were given the means to save by allowing them to make extra profits, and they had the incentive to save the money for the simple reason that they were unable to spend it.

PAYING FOR THE WAR

So long as the war lasted the various belligerent governments were well enough content to carry on by the help of such expedients as happened to present themselves. When the war was over, however, it became necessary to meet the demands of the bondholders for the payment of interest.

Financially speaking the war had placed the pensioner and the bondholder in an improved position and had made them entitled to larger portions of the national wealth, but for the bondholder to have secured an increased share of the national wealth would have involved a social revolution, and such a result is not easily realised in practice.

In a modern democratic state the wage-earner has a large measure of political power and he is in a position to resist any serious alteration in his standard of living. On the other hand trade assets have a way of reverting sooner or later to their real value in spite of influences which may temporarily interfere with the process. The bondholder's efforts to secure the interest which had been promised to him may therefore be likened to attempts to squeeze the upper and the nether millstones. In the end he was compelled to accept much the same share of the national income as he had always done, but the actual procedure by which this result was reached is instructive.

To repudiate the bondholders' claims would of

course have been dishonest, and any government which suggested such a proceeding would no doubt have been overwhelmed in a storm of disapproval. Other methods, less direct and therefore easier, but none the less effective, were however available.

Most governments began by paying the interest on their war loans with borrowed money, and they continued to pursue this simple expedient for so long as they could find people sufficiently confiding to lend to them. After a time lenders began to realise that they were simply paying themselves their own interest, and confidence evaporated. No more loans were forthcoming and the governments were driven to adopt the final expedient which is always available to governments which are unable to meet their obligations. They printed more paper money, inflated the currency and wiped out the bondholders' claims just as effectively as if they had repudiated them.

In case it should be thought that the bondholder was treated with undue hardship, however, it may be well to observe that the whole position created by the war was extremely artificial. The money which had been spent was represented by no tangible assets. There were no buildings or machinery to increase the production of industry such as would exist in the case of commercial investments. Quite literally the whole of the assets had gone up in smoke.

In addition to this the people who had "saved" money during the war had not done so from any special motives of thrift. In most cases they saved simply because they could not help it.

While sympathising with cases of individual hardship therefore it is difficult to see that the ultimate outcome could be other than it actually was.

GREAT BRITAIN'S SOLUTION

While continental countries were dealing with their bondholders after the manner already described, Great Britain was evolving a characteristic solution of her own.

A considerable part of the cost of the war had already been paid out of taxes, and high taxation was therefore accepted with less reluctance. At the same time the machinery for reducing the bondholder's income was already in existence.

Income tax and death duties are paid by the well-to-do, and it was merely necessary to raise them to an appropriate figure in order to provide the money required to pay the bondholder's claim to additional interest. In effect, the investor in his role of taxpayer hands over a proportion of his income to the tax collector. The government then takes this money and pays it back to the taxpayer as interest on his war loan, and the investor or taxpayer whichever we like to call him is in just the same position as if there were no war loan and no income tax. A wonderful device, is it not?

Without departing from the path of strict financial rectitude, Great Britain was thus able to cancel the bondholder's claim to a larger share of the national income. The ultimate result was the same, but the disturbances which accompany an inflation of the currency were avoided. By 1923, five years after the war, it may I think be said that matters in Great Britain had returned more or less to normal. So far as can be judged by appearances it might be said that the general standard of living throughout Great Britain was very much the same as it had been before the war.

THE LESSON OF WAR FINANCE

Looking back over the whole period of the war and the period of reconstruction which followed it, there seems to be one principle which stands out clearly, and that is the fundamental conservatism of human nature. A social structure which has been gradually developed in the course of generations is not readily disturbed. The functions and emoluments of different classes in the community are fixed by habit and custom, and the form of structure thus created involves a certain distribution of wealth between the different classes.

The lesson to be learnt is that the social structure and its associated distribution of wealth offer very great resistance to forces which tend to produce any radical change. A disturbance may produce some temporary readjustment, but it will certainly provoke reactions which will in the long run restore the situation to normal.

CHAPTER XVI

REPARATIONS AND WAR DEBTS

THE THREE PROBLEMS

FROM the economic standpoint reparations and war debts have the same characteristics and give rise to the same three problems—how the debtor is to find the money, how the money is to be paid, and what the creditor is to do with the money when he has got it.

At the time of writing (1933) the question of reparations has passed through the first two phases, which may be said to cover the world's struggles towards a solution of the first two problems. Or perhaps it would be more accurate to describe the events which have taken place as the struggles of a disillusioned world towards the hard truth that the problems are to a great extent insoluble.

As regards the first problem it will be observed that reparations and war debts are the international counterpart of war loans: they tend to alter the distribution of wealth and increase the claim of the bondholders to the detriment of trade and industry. As already explained, war loans have been almost entirely cancelled either by inflation of the currency or by the imposition of a high rate of income tax, and it is certainly unfortunate that it has not been possible to deal with reparations and war debts by equally expeditious methods.

It is also instructive to note that the scaling down of reparations which has actually taken place has been due in greater measure to the difficulties which have arisen in regard to the question of exchange rather than the question of the debtor's taxable capacity.

THE PEACE TREATY AND ITS CONSEQUENCES

The long sad story of ignorance and futility which is known by the title of Reparations and War Debts has been often set out by abler pens than mine, and it is unnecessary to repeat it in detail here. (24)

The Treaty of Versailles laid down the principle that Germany was liable for all the damage which had been suffered by the Allies, and a Reparations Committee was appointed to work out the money value of this obligation. It carried out its work in due course and placed the required figure at £6,600 millions, and it was on this basis that early attempts were made to effect a settlement.

The allied statesmen were warned by Mr. J. M. Keynes (25) and other economists that these enormous figures were impossible of realisation, but the warnings fell on deaf ears.

Within a period agreeing very closely with the predictions of the economists the inevitable occurred, and German currency collapsed. The occupation of the Ruhr followed.

The next step was the appointment of the Dawes Committee and the tacit admission that the payment demanded must bear some relation to the debtor's capacity to pay. The committee survived for about five years, and gave the world a very valuable breathing space, but it did not solve the problem of reparations.

In any case the powers given to the Dawes Committee were of a provisional character, and it was felt that an effort should be made to arrive at a final settlement of the whole problem. A new committee was therefore appointed with revised terms of reference.

The Young Committee had been in existence for two years when the financial collapse of 1931 brought matters to a crisis, and the further payment of reparations became impossible.

HOW REPARATIONS WERE PAID

During the twelve years which followed the signing of the treaty Germany paid certain sums in reparations.

It was believed by those who drafted the treaty and the various agreements which succeeded it that a return to normal conditions would enable Germany to create an export trade by means of which the reparations would be paid. In actual fact, however, no such export trade was ever established. Germany was able to borrow from her former enemies, not only enough to pay the reparations which were demanded of her, but a good deal more as well.

In the early years the money was obtained from speculators who believed that the mark would eventually recover, which of course it did not. After the collapse of the mark and the establishment of a new German currency on a gold basis, money was obtained from abroad by means of loans and similar expedients of international finance. The total sums borrowed in this way were nearly double the amount paid back in reparations.

To cut a long story short Germany has never paid any reparations except on paper. It would be a great deal nearer the truth to say that other countries during the past ten years have been paying reparations to Germany. Truly a Gilbertian situation.

AN OPPORTUNITY MISSED

What makes the whole business the more regrettable is that a sound solution of the reparations problem was available and was in fact very nearly adopted.

The greater part of the fighting took place in the north-east corner of France and the rebuilding of this devastated area was one of the first tasks which had to be faced on the conclusion of peace. The task was a reasonable one and would have been willingly accepted by the German people. The German building trade had the necessary men and the necessary materials, which the French had not. The scheme was supported by the French Labour Organisations. Apparently every condition was favourable. Above all the work would have been paid for in German currency and no exchange difficulty would have arisen.

If the scheme had been adopted the currency collapses in Germany and France might have been avoided, or at least their severity would have been reduced, and the world at large would have been saved a decade of chaos and readjustment.

Unfortunately the French building trade objected, and political prejudice no doubt played its part. The scheme failed to materialise. The French building trade made its profits, but the houses took three times as long to build and cost three or four times as much. (26)

The golden opportunity was missed.

THE FUNDAMENTAL ERROR

The various discussions which took place in regard to reparations were all carried on in terms of money. The ultimate effect on trade of the decisions which were arrived at was never really faced at all.

Now foreign trade consists in fact of the transfer of commodities, and money is simply a form of accounting which represents one, but only one, of the various aspects of these international transactions.

"There is no clearer indication than the history of reparations of the way in which monetary expressions cloak the real physical facts behind them, and if people realised the facts about the transfer of goods from one national heap to another, they would appreciate the real underlying difficulties of the situation." (27)

The essential problem to which the energies of the allied statesmen and their experts should have been devoted was the question of ascertaining what types of commodity the creditor countries were in a position to accept. The questions of Germany's taxable capacity and her ability to manufacture goods for export were relevant but of secondary importance.

The fundamental error was that the allied statesmen endeavoured to work out the problem in terms of money instead of doing so in terms of commodities. Account keeping is a necessary factor in the modern commercial structure, but, if one is to avoid being misled by appearances, it is essential to look below the surface and study the movements of commodities which are only dimly revealed in their monetary aspects.

THE EFFECT OF FOREIGN LOANS

There is, I think, a second lesson to be learned from the reparations fiasco.

I have already drawn attention to the fact that excessive flexibility in any structure may accentuate fluctuations instead of controlling them, and I think the principle is clearly apparent in the present instance.

If Germany had been unable to borrow money abroad the realities of the situation would surely have thrust themselves on the notice of the allied statesmen in the course of two or three years at most. The fog of mystery which has obscured the whole business would have been dispersed a decade earlier than it was, and the blind groping along a false trail, with its sad story of wasted effort, might have been avoided.

WAR DEBTS

At the time of writing (1933) there are not wanting signs that the question of reparations is approaching a final settlement, but the question of war debts still remains the subject of acute controversy.

It is unlikely that the wage-earners of the debtor nations will submit to any reduction of their standard of living, and it is impossible that the burden should be placed on trade and industry, so that the burden, if it is to be borne at all, must be placed on the shoulders of the bondholders.

Whether the debtor nations will be able to devise methods by which this may be accomplished I shall not venture to say. The problem is not rendered easier by the fact that the debts are being continuously increased owing to the rise in the value of gold, a contingency which was not foreseen or provided for when the debts were contracted.

Passing from this aspect of the matter, and assuming that the debtor nations are able to shoulder these debts either in whole or in part, we come to the second problem, how they are to be paid.

Payment in the form of special services is not possible, and an adjustment of the debt through the medium of trade balances is the only alternative. If creditor countries maintain their tariffs and thereby prevent an increase of imports, it is evident that this balance can only be obtained by a contraction of exports, and it seems to be further evident that this loss of trade will give rise to a corresponding loss of employment.

It would appear therefore that the first signs of a trade revival are to be looked for among the debtor countries rather than among the creditors.

Finally we come to the last of our three problems, the question what the creditor will do with the money when he gets it. At first sight it may appear that this is not a problem at all, but it is to be remembered that the benefits of this influx of wealth are not equally distributed; they pass to that particular class in the community which I have referred to as the bondholders.

The low rates of interest now prevailing tend to show that the volume of savings is at present adequate for all the legitimate demands of trade and industry. The payment of international obligations such as reparations and war debts would certainly increase the volume of savings in creditor countries, and might possibly create a surplus which trade and industry would be unable to absorb. In that case the effect of the excess of savings might be to bring a strong pressure to bear on the banks to buy gold as the only possible means of disposing of an ever-increasing volume of deposits.

We are told that it is hard for a rich man to enter into the Kingdom of Heaven. It is also very difficult for a rich man to spend his money in such a manner that it shall be of real benefit both to himself and to the community, and it will be interesting to see whether the creditor countries are capable of discovering a solution to this complex and difficult problem.

CHAPTER XVII

GREAT BRITAIN'S RETURN TO THE GOLD STANDARD

THE VARIOUS ALTERNATIVES

THE advantages of the gold standard in facilitating international trade are well known, and it was natural that Great Britain, who had abandoned the gold standard during the war, should endeavour to return to it.

There remained however the important question of deciding on the value of the pound sterling in terms of gold. Broadly speaking three courses were possible:—

(i) To re-establish the pound on the same gold basis as that which existed before the war.

(ii) To accept the actual exchange value of the pound sterling in those countries which had retained the gold standard. This would have meant that the gold value of the new pound would have been about nine-tenths the value of the old one. (28)

(iii) To use the price level of commodities as the basis for the new value of the pound. This would have fixed the pound at about two-thirds the value of the old one. (29)

The arguments in favour of the first course of action, which was actually adopted, may be summed up as follows:—

(*a*) There was believed to be a moral or legal obligation to return to the gold standard on the pre-war basis as soon as this step was practically feasible.

(*b*) A reduction in the value of the pound would cause loss of prestige and would injure Great Britain's position as an international banker.

(*c*) A reduction in the value of the pound would increase the debt which would have to be paid by Europe to the United States.

(*d*) A reduction in the value of the pound would reduce the value of Great Britain's foreign investments.

The only one of these arguments on which I shall comment is the last, and in this connection I shall remind the reader of the parable of the unjust steward. The interpretation of this parable has I believe caused considerable difficulty to theologians, but its meaning should be clear enough to the business man. The moral is that a creditor can never get more than the debtor is able to pay. If he accepts this amount willingly he will lose nothing in money, and will retain the debtor's good will, which is in itself an asset of considerable value.

However I have digressed somewhat and I must return to the story.

THE DECISION AND ITS RESULTS

Great Britain actually decided to return to the gold standard on the pre-war basis. Steps were taken to raise the exchange value of the pound, and in due course the stage was set, and in March 1925 the deed was done.

The consequences of this step were twofold.

In the home market the rise in the value of money produced the effects described in the last chapter. The earnings of the industrialist and the trader were reduced and profits dissolved into losses. (30)

At the same time the costs of production were reflected in the prices of exports and the export trade declined, and it is estimated by Mr. Keynes that the loss of wealth amounted to about £100,000,000 a year over a period of several years. (31)

In the industrial world the loss of profits naturally provoked an intense struggle between employer and employed, but it is unnecessary to describe in detail the incidents of this contest. As between the combatants honours were fairly evenly divided, for what the wage-earner lost in unemployment the investor lost in reduced dividends.

The ultimate outcome of the struggle was probably inevitable although matters might have drifted on longer than they did if the world crisis had not brought them to a head. The strains provoked by the crisis, however, revealed the fact that the bond-holder's enhanced claim was inconsistent with the accepted structure of society, and Great Britain was driven off the gold standard. The pound sterling has fallen to a figure approximating closely to what it would have been if it had been fixed on a commodity basis, and the bondholder's claim to an enhanced share of the national dividend has been cancelled.

The whole incident furnishes an instructive example of the troubles which follow from any policy which gives the bondholder a claim to an abnormal share of the national dividend. The lesson has been an expensive one, and it is to be hoped that it will not soon be forgotten.

THE EFFECT OF GREAT BRITAIN'S FINANCIAL STRENGTH

The whole incident of Great Britain's return to the gold standard is also instructive in another way. As a result of the handicap of high wages and high fixed costs the export trade declined at a continually increasing rate. Under normal conditions Great Britain has a surplus of savings which is invested abroad. The first effect of the declining export trade was to reduce this surplus gradually to vanishing point, and finally Great Britain, with all her magnificent industrial equipment, was reduced to the position of a borrower in the world's markets. No longer producing what she required to fill her own needs she was reduced to depending on the charity of other nations who were kind enough or foolish enough to lend to her. (32)

Ultimately lenders became frightened and Great Britain was driven off the gold standard. Far from being an asset to her, Great Britain's financial strength was really a disadvantage, for it prolonged an impossible position and postponed the inevitable day of reckoning. It would have been much better if the financial system had been less flexible and Great Britain had been compelled to correct her error two or three years earlier than was actually the case.

CHAPTER XVIII

THE CAUSES OF THE CRISIS

ULTIMATE CAUSES

EVERY industrial crisis of any magnitude is certainly due to a combination of different causes, and it is also certain that the various factors involved act and react upon each other, so that the whole problem is essentially complex. Looking at the matter from the broadest standpoint, however, the outstanding feature on which it is necessary to focus our attention is that the industrial and financial structure contains elements which tend to produce instability.

The stability of a mechanical structure depends also upon a number of factors such as weight, height and so on, and it is the business of the designer to see that no individual factor is allowed to attain such importance as to endanger the safety of the whole edifice.

A particular wall for example may be perfectly well able to withstand any storm which is likely to strike it, and it may even be possible to raise it to a certain extent without serious risk. It is certain, however, that each increase in height reduces its margin of stability, and, if it is raised repeatedly, a point will ultimately be reached when the factor of safety becomes inadequate. In due course the storm comes, and the wall collapses. Thoughtless people may attribute the destruction of the wall to the storm, but prudent men will take the lesson to heart and will design their walls with larger factors of safety.

And so it is with the elaborate industrial and financial structure which has gradually envolved itself in the modern world. Its stability depends upon a number of factors which are more or less under human control, and the growth of particular elements to an extent which renders the whole edifice unstable can properly be regarded as the ultimate causes of the actual failure.

Some of the more important sources of weakness are described in the following sections; some of them evidently originated in the industrial and financial disturbances connected with the Great War, but the war cannot be blamed for the whole of the trouble. In the years which have elapsed since the Armistice efforts should have been directed towards broadening the base of the economic structure and making it more stable; in actual fact financial expedients have been devised which have raised it higher and higher, and rendered it less and less stable, and less and less fitted to bear the shocks of financial disturbance and lack of confidence.

In the end the storm has come and the whole affair has collapsed like a house of cards.

The war ended in 1918, and a period of five or

six years should have been adequate for the essential work of reconstruction. The critical period may be said to comprise the years 1924 to 1929 or thereabouts, and it is convenient to fix our attention on the events which occurred and the policies which were followed during that important time.

THE LACK OF BALANCE BETWEEN IMPORTS AND EXPORTS

In the years preceding the war America was developing more rapidly than Europe and there was a perfectly legitimate flow of trade and investment from Europe to America. The war brought this to an end, and gave rise to a great flow of commodities from America to Europe, so that, under the stimulus of the war, the United States became a great exporting nation, and the pre-war balance of imports became a balance of exports.

Now this balance of exports was not paid for in gold, for the very good reason that the importers did not possess the gold for the purpose. In other words, the commodities were exported on a credit basis, the credit taking the form partly of investments and partly of short term loans. Now it is clear that the repayment of debts cannot be postponed for ever, and it should have been obvious that the question would eventually arise as to how and when this constantly rising volume of debt could be repaid.

If the United States were to become involved in a war outside Europe, a flow of commodities from

Europe to America would no doubt be welcomed, and the debt could be paid. Apart from this rather remote contingency, however, it is difficult to foresee any situation in which a large balance of imports would be accepted by the farmers and the wage-earners of the United States; and, if it is not acceptable at the present time, there is no reason to suppose that it will become any more acceptable in the future.

But if this proposition is accepted, it follows that there is no reasonable probability that Europe will ever be able to repay its debts to America, and it further follows that the continuance of the export of commodities from America to Europe was unjustified. In the interest of general stability it was necessary that it should cease, and the sooner the better.

And this was not all. At the time referred to Europe was considerably in debt to America both on private and on government accounts. If these debts were to be discharged it was not sufficient to secure a balance between imports and exports; it was necessary for the United States to go further and establish an import balance corresponding to the amount of debt which it was agreed should be paid.

A similar argument, but in an opposite sense, applied to Germany. It had been settled in the peace treaties that Germany was to pay reparations (the question of the amount need not concern us for the moment), and it was necessary that she should establish an export balance for that purpose.

These maladjustments of the trade balance were sources of instability to the whole financial structure, and it should have been the business of those concerned to correct them.

TARIFFS AND SUBSIDIES

As already explained tariffs and shipping subsidies have the effect of reducing imports, and may be legitimately employed in correcting the balance of trade when a country is importing too much and is drifting into debt.

The war created a number of new states, however, and these states initiated tariff barriers for political or other reasons without adequate consideration of the actual and potential effects on the balance of trade. Since political, military and economic factors cannot be reduced to any common basis, it is impossible to express an opinion as to the desirability or otherwise of these changes.

The chief failure to appreciate the significance of the trade balance occurred, however, in the United States where the changes were presumably made for purely economic reasons. At a time when tariffs should have been lowered so as to reduce the unjustifiable excess of exports, and pave the way for the payment of European war debts, tariffs and shipping subsidies were introduced which decreased the importation of commodities from Europe instead of increasing it.

Great Britain's return to the gold standard also

aggravated the situation. Great Britain has always been widely interested in the development of backward countries and normally maintains an export balance for that purpose. The curtailment of this export balance and its eventual reversal had no justification, and facilitated the expansion of the American export balance already referred to.

THE FAILURE OF THE AUTOMATIC CONTROL OF THE TRADE BALANCE

Before the weakness of the system was revealed by the present crisis, it was believed by economists that economic forces were in themselves adequate to control any situation that might arise, and that these forces would compel traders and industrialists to adopt policies which would speedily correct any lack of adjustment in the balance of trade. In fact, however, nothing of the sort took place.

The import balance of Germany which should have changed into an export balance showed no such tendency.

The export balance of the United States of America, which on several separate accounts should have contracted, showed a tendency to expand.

Exports from Great Britain, which might have been expected to show a modest increase, fell heavily.

For about six years the looked-for control failed to act, and, when it did act, it acted with such abruptness and severity that the whole system was thrown out of joint.

The reason for this failure will be clear from what has already been said in Chapter XIII. Lack of balance between imports and exports can go on just so long as the exporting country is prepared to part with goods on credit, and no longer; when foreign investment and foreign short term lending cease, the trade balance is automatically and inevitably reduced to zero. In other words flexibility in the trade balance is governed by flexibility in foreign lending, and those who provide the money for foreign loans have the power of controlling the trade balance, and do in fact control it, whether they realise their responsibilities or not.

The maladjustments of various trade balances, already described in the previous section, were therefore rendered possible by the willingness of various people to lend money abroad in one form or another, and it was this willingness to lend which delayed and aggravated the crisis. In fact one may go further and say that an earlier commencement of the crisis would not only have rendered the crisis itself less severe, but would have revealed the unsoundness of the policy of tariffs and subsidies before the damage done had become irreparable.

In a literal sense the factors which caused the lack of balance between imports and exports may be regarded as ultimate causes of the crisis, but this is not the aspect of the matter which is usually uppermost in men's minds when the crisis comes to be discussed. It is rather the abruptness of the change and the consequent dislocation of trade and industry which assume the more serious importance. It is in this connection that foreign investment and foreign short term lending become the controlling factors and take their place as essential causes in the production of the crisis.

OVER-EXPANSION OF THE MEANS OF PRODUCTION

The war gave a great stimulus to mass production methods, and there was a strong tendency towards the increased usc of such methods in established industries, of which agriculture was perhaps the chief example. To a considerable extent such tendencies were probably beyond human control, but an already difficult position was aggravated in various directions by tariffs and subsidies.

The secondary effect of tariffs and subsidies being to cause a surplus of the means of production, the increase in the means of production due to the widespread adoption of mass production methods was augmented by the reactions due to these tariffs and subsidies.

An example will perhaps make this point clearer. For the purpose of illustration let us assume, what is not indeed very far from the truth, that in the period immediately following the war shipping services rendered to the United States by Great Britain were balanced by the export of American motor-cars. The introduction of the shipping subsidies has created an American mercantile marine, and Great Britain has found herself with a surplus of ships and a surplus of shipbuilding facilities. The trade balance having reasserted its importance, the United States has now lost its export trade in motor-cars and Europe is busily engaged in duplicating the motor-car factories which already exist in the United States.

Thus, the introduction of the shipping subsidies has created a surplus of ships, a surplus of shipbuilding facilities, and a surplus of motor-car factories, and it is small wonder that trade and industry have been upset by these upheavals.

OVER-PRODUCTION

It is an old saying that misfortunes seldom come singly, and whatever truth the proverb may contain in regard to life in general there is no doubt about its truth in relation to trade and industry. The collapse of one important group of industries throws out of employment a number of work-people and reduces or destroys their power of spending. This in turn upsets the balance between production and consumption and provokes a production slump of the type which has already been described in Chapter IX.

The investment slump may be regarded as the primary cause of the crisis, but its intensity has been aggravated by the inherent instability of the combined structure of which industry, trade and finance are the component parts.

The instability of this structure and the consequent slump in production must therefore be regarded as having contributed in no small degree to the severity of the crisis.

The trouble has been aggravated by ill-conceived attempts to hoard surplus supplies instead of reducing production.

OVER-EXPANSION OF CREDIT

Expansion of credit stimulates and facilitates legitimate trade and enterprise, it stimulates unsound investment, and it provokes speculation in stocks and shares, and, whether sound or otherwise, it leaves behind a burden of debt which undermines the stability of the whole financial structure.

Over-expansion of credit has been particularly conspicuous in America, where speculation attained such dimensions that it appears to have dwarfed the operations of legitimate trade and industry. (33)

THE GOLD STANDARD

As already explained in Chapter VI a rise in the value of money, or if we prefer to call it so a fall in the prices of commodities, gives to the bondholder a claim to a larger share of the national income. Or if we pass from the national to the international theatre of events, a general rise in the value of money gives to bondholders all over the world a claim to a larger share of the world's income.

In the province of engineering it is well known

that any member of a structure will fail if it is stressed beyond its elastic limit. It is perhaps less fully recognised that debtors can also be pressed beyond the breaking point, although the lesson seems to be repeated with unfailing regularity in successive generations. If the bondholder's claim is increased by changes in the value of money, some of the weaker debtors will be driven out of business, and matters will only be stabilised again by cancelling some part of the excessive burden.

As regards the actual changes in the value of gold it is recorded that the change in value has twice been as much as 40 per cent in twenty-five years, and since the war it has risen nearly 20 per cent in five years. (34) Recent events do not appear to suggest that the end of the rise is yet in sight.

I will not venture to estimate what part the rising value of money has played in the present crisis, for the causes already mentioned would probably have been adequate in themselves to provoke a crisis of some sort. It is sufficient to observe that a currency which is constantly increasing in value is a source of instability, and that equilibrium is only attained under such conditions by periodical financial revolutions.

SUMMARY

The principal causes of the crisis may now be summarised as follows:—

1. A lack of balance in certain countries between

imports and exports, which may be attributed in part to the war, in part to tariffs and subsidies, and in part to unjustifiable foreign investment and foreign short term lending.

2. Over-expansion of the means of production in many industries, which may be attributed in part to the introduction of mass production methods, in part to unwise investment, but mainly to the secondary effects of the tariffs and subsidies already referred to.

3. Over-production in many industries, to be attributed to the causes referred to in the previous paragraph.

4. The over-expansion of credit under conditions which should have indicated that the need of the moment was caution rather than optimism.

5. The fall in world prices due to the increasing value of gold, which may be attributed in part to the increasing cost of gold production, and in part to the fact that badly controlled currency policies have caused the demand for gold to outrun the supply.

In the next chapter I shall endeavour to fix responsibility for these various causes of instability in the economic structure, and suggestions will be made as to how similar troubles might be minimised in the future.

CHAPTER XIX

THE LESSONS OF THE CRISIS

THE SIGNIFICANCE OF THE TRADE BALANCE

APART from gold movements, differences between imports and exports are necessarily balanced by loans and investments, and a serious lack of balance can be sustained only so long as investors believe that the investments will be profitable and that the loans will ultimately be repaid. The condition of the trade balances is therefore one of the most important factors which influence the stability of international trade, and their proper control is an essential element in the prosperity of the nations individually and collectively.

The actual policies adopted during the past fifteen years show no indication that this elementary economic principle had ever been heard of, still less that its importance had been appreciated.

The settlements made in the peace treaties studiously avoided the issue, and France refused to accept the only rational solution of the reparations problem.

Great Britain in her turn adopted a money policy which led to a continuous loss of exports and expansion of imports until she was nearly driven into bankruptcy.

But the most glaring case is provided by the United

States of America. Over a period of years when there was a quite unjustifiable balance of exports, politicians vied with each other in devising means for upsetting the balance still further. If tariffs and subsidies had been introduced before the war when the United States imports exceeded exports no exception could be taken to such measures; they would have been perfectly reasonable. In the conditions actually existing every increase in the tariff and every dollar spent on shipping subsidies was a nail in the coffin of the export trade and a definite step towards the final disaster.

Nor is the dislocation of international trade the only consequence of these mistaken policies. They have led to the building of more ships and the construction of more factories than the world requires, and the industries which centre about the building of ships and the construction of factories must remain idle until the lapse of time enables the surplus to be absorbed.

It has already been pointed out, and it cannot be too strongly emphasised, that the least important consequence of such errors is the loss of the investor's money. An equally serious matter is the loss of confidence which discourages progress and restricts legitimate enterprise. But by far the most serious result is the effect which misdirected investment produces upon the course of industrial development.

The development of any industry involves the training of a vast army of work-people whose means of livelihood depends upon the continuation of the particular industry in which they are employed. If the enterprise collapses this army of contented and industrious citizens becomes unemployed and perhaps unemployable.

In such matters it is futile to blame economists and politicians. Every individual citizen who has cast his vote in favour of this undesirable increase of tariffs must share the responsibility, and can thank himself for the losses which he has himself sustained during the crisis.

THE INVESTOR TAKES A WRONG TURNING

The next person who must accept a share of responsibility for the crisis is the investor.

During the war and the period of reconstruction which followed it, the insistent demand for investment money had maintained the rate of interest on the best securities at about 5 per cent., and investors, in which term I include bankers, business men, stockbrokers and the general public, had gradually acquired what may be called a 5 per cent. complex. They had learned to look for a high rate of interest, the need for security was temporarily forgotten, and investment proceeded on lines which were thoroughly unsound.

In the first place money was lent to foreign countries who showed no prospect of being able to discharge their debts in the form of any commodity which the creditor would be able to accept.

In the second place money was invested in enterprises of such a type that the effect was to increase the means of production at a greater rate than could be justified by actual and potential consumption. Much of the foreign lending did in fact produce this kind of result.

The investor's contribution to the crisis is therefore fairly clear. He has displayed a lack of judgement, and has employed his money in directions which were fundamentally unsound. The realisation of these errors has provoked an investment slump, which is, as already explained, a much more serious matter than a production slump, and takes a much longer time to correct.

The distinction between class A and class B investments in foreign countries has already been referred to and may be summarised here. Briefly speaking the characteristics of sound or class A foreign investments are as follows:—

Firstly, the money should be spent on the development of enterprises of a reproductive character, and the lender should take steps to ensure that the agreed policy is actually translated into practice. A change of government is sometimes regarded as an adequate excuse for the repudiation of international promises, and the stability of the government and the national record for honest dealing are matters which have to be taken into consideration.

Secondly, the commodity which the enterprise is designed to produce should be one which the lending country is unable to produce in adequate quantities for itself, so that payment can be made by the transfer of this commodity. The condition must of course be interpreted in a liberal sense so as not to exclude such enterprises as railways, which may be regarded as part of the national workshop, and which may be paid for by the transfer of appropriate commodities in the production and marketing of which the railway will no doubt have played an essential part.

More complex arrangements involving the exchange of commodities with other countries are not excluded but evidently require careful and detailed examination before they are accepted as appropriate.

Thirdly, provision should be made for an adequate sinking fund so that the repayment of capital and interest may be secured before the utility of the enterprise has evaporated. In this connection I cannot help feeling that the accepted practice of separating the payment of interest from the repayment of capital is open to serious objections. I venture to suggest, for the consideration of those who deal with such matters, that it would be more satisfactory to arrange for repayment in the form of a terminable annuity which would embrace both capital and interest.

Fourthly, competition between lenders is extremely objectionable. If it is found to exist it should be eliminated by international agreement.

Fifthly, the debtor's burden should not be artificially increased by changes in the real value of national or international currencies.

Compliance with the first four conditions suggests that greater caution is desirable in future in regard to foreign investment but involves no serious departure from existing practice. How the fifth condition is to be complied with is a much more difficult question to which I shall not attempt to provide a definite answer.

It raises the question of devising some form of currency which will not be subject to a continuous rise in value, with a consequent depression of the price level. Apart from this particular difficulty, it may be presumed that investors will profit by the lessons which have been so dearly bought, and it is to be expected that greater care will be exercised in future.

FOREIGN SHORT TERM LENDING

The significance of foreign short term lending as a factor in the crisis has already been explained, and it is well known that the volume of short term foreign lending did expand considerably in the momentous years which preceded the crisis.

Text-books on Economics often identify the volume of short term lending with the volume of working capital in trade and industry, and it may be agreed that a large amount of short term lending is employed for the purpose indicated. The suggested relationship is also I think an accepted principle of banking policy, and the item "Advances to Customers" in a bank balance sheet is supposed to indicate assets of this character.

The position with regard to foreign short term loans is not quite clear, but it is to be presumed that there would be general agreement that these loans should also be made against assets of a similar type.

The disclosures which have taken place in the course of the crisis, however, have made it evident that the admirable principle that short term loans should be made only on the security of short term obligations has been honoured in the breach rather than in the observance. The banker has devised the convenient phrase that his assets have become "frozen." It would be more accurate to say quite simply that loans have been made without adequate and appropriate security, and that they have met with the fate which might be expected from financial operations of this character. There is no doubt that the ultimate security for a great volume of so-called short term assets has been, not working capital, but foreign investments of a type which could not be regarded as satisfactory even as investments.

There is yet another aspect of the business of foreign lending which demands serious attention, and that is the number of intermediaries who appear in connection with transactions of this character, thereby disguising the character of the security which is being offered and the nature of the risks which are being run.

When a private investor holds government bonds or the shares of an industrial company, the extent of the risk may be difficult to estimate, but its character is clearly defined. With short term loans on the other hand it seldom occurs that there is any such direct relationship between the original lender and the ultimate borrower.

The money may be provided in the first instance by a business man who deposits his hard-earned savings in some bank believing that he is thereby securing himself against loss of capital. The bank in turn may lend the money on short term conditions to some foreign bank, and this foreign bank may in its turn lend the money to some industrialist who employs the money in the erection of a factory, the final loan being entered into in the belief that the enterprise is sound and that it will be possible in due course to repay the loan by issuing shares to the investing public. In this instance the ultimate security for the depositor's money is a foreign factory the investment in which probably fails to satisfy the necessary conditions for sound foreign investment.

Here then is a weak spot in the modern financial system which evidently demands reform, although my criticism in the matter must not be misunderstood. I am not suggesting that bankers and international financiers have entered into a conspiracy which enables them to throw into confusion the industrial system of the world and draw their ill-gotten profits from the seething cauldron of their fellow creatures' misfortunes. It is not my desire to portray any such witches' kitchen. I suggest merely that the system of international finance which has gradually evolved itself is no longer appropriate to the world situation which exists at the present time.

It would be wrong in fact to suppose that the banks have complete control over foreign lending, and the transfer of private deposits from one country to another is known to have played a large part in particular spasms of the present crisis.

How foreign short term lending can be controlled and restricted is a problem the solution of which is neither easy nor obvious; nevertheless it is evident that the problem is one which will have to be solved if international trade is to attain a reasonable measure of stability.

As a preliminary step what would suggest itself is that each country should establish a bank for international exchange, or at least a branch of some existing bank, which would deal exclusively with all transactions involving foreign exchange. This institution would become in fact the clearing house for foreign exchange, and would be the channel through which all foreign exchange would flow.

The first advantage of such an arrangement would be that the ordinary records of the exchange bank would provide the much needed information as to the general trend of foreign exchange transactions. They ought to reveal, much sooner than is possible at present, any objectionable tendency which it might be desirable to check.

In some cases the necessary remedies may lie in the field of national policy or banking practice, and may be capable of correction by accepted methods. In other cases some measure of control might suggest itself, and in that case the exchange bank would provide a good deal of the machinery which would be required for the purpose. In short the exchange bank would serve a double purpose, it would show up any undesirable tendencies, and it would at the same time strengthen available methods of dealing with them.

Finally, if the country remained off the gold standard, the exchange bank would provide traders with their present and future requirements in foreign currencies.

With the existence of the exchange bank it would presumably be possible to differentiate between the rates of interest for foreign and internal short term credits respectively. One of the difficulties of the present system is that the central bank may desire to contract foreign credit and expand home credit, or *vice versa* (35), but under existing conditions any such distinction is impossible. With the concentration of all foreign exchange transactions in the hands of a single institution it ought to be possible to overcome this limitation.

There appear, therefore, to be very strong reasons for reform in the direction which has been indicated.

THE BANKS AND THE CRISIS

It is generally agreed that the banks are able to influence, to a considerable extent, the expansion and contraction of credit, and the question naturally arises as to whether this power has been wisely used and whether it is desirable that it should be increased or diminished.

Banking practice differs widely in different countries. In Great Britain small banks have gradually been absorbed by their larger neighbours until there have remained only a very small number of large and powerful institutions, and these act in very close combination and upon mutually agreed principles, so that it may be said that Great Britain possesses a single banking system rather than a number of separate banks. In the United States on the other hand there still exist thousands of small banks acting independently and liable to fail whenever unusual stress is brought to bear on some particular section of the community. The British system has many obvious advantages, and in particular the bankers' assets are distributed throughout the whole community and are not endangered by local and sectional disturbances.

The American banking system is still in the course of evolution and will no doubt tend to approximate more closely to British practice in this respect. Banking failures in the United States have been a source of considerable embarrassment during the present crisis.

There is also a wide difference in various countries in regard to the nature of the assets in which the banks' money is invested. It is often the practice to allow a considerable proportion of the assets to be tied up in the form of industrial investments, and it has been claimed that this system has the advantage that it gives greater assistance to industry. On the other hand industrial investments are inconsistent with the banker's obligation to refund his customers' deposits in cash, and this difficulty has taken very practical shape in Germany, Austria and elsewhere. It seems much better that banking and industrial investment should be clearly separated, and this appears to be one of the lessons which may be learnt from the present crisis.

The question of trade cycles has already been alluded to. The banker's ability to reduce the severity of these disturbances evidently depends on two things; firstly, his ability to foresee possible sources of trouble, and secondly the power to take effective action when he believes such action to be desirable. This problem has already been the subject of much discussion amongst bankers and economists, and it is too intricate and too controversial for discussion here. It is sufficient to remark that the banks do take such measures as they believe to be in the public interest, and that better control can only be expected in the light of greater knowledge and as the result of further study and research.

There is, however, one matter of banking policy which is evidently related to the present crisis and which is obviously open to criticism, and that is the action of the Federal Reserve Banks in assisting the expansion of credit in the United States in 1927.

The abnormal expansion of internal credit in the United States has been severely criticised by economists in that country (36), and it is obvious that it did much to contribute to the instability of the whole financial structure, but it is by no means obvious that the credit structures would have broken down if other causes of instability had been absent.

In the year 1925 the position in regard to international trade balances was thoroughly unsound, and it continued to deteriorate steadily from that time onwards. I think it may justly be said that the world's bankers should have realised the significance of this factor and should have taken steps to minimise its effects.

To put the matter quite simply, the time selected for the expansion of credit was inopportune. Bankers and economists should have warned the politicians of the danger, and should have indicated the way in which it was being increased by subsidies and tariffs. At the same time they should have restricted credit as far as possible until such time as the trade balances were brought more nearly into adjustment.

In actual fact the expansion of credit in the

United States did much to promote unsound foreign lending of all kinds, and thus postponed and aggravated the crisis. It also led to a great deal of speculation in stocks and shares, an effect which is very undesirable from every point of view.

The reduction of speculation of this type is one of the problems which arises in connection with the crisis, but the correct solution is by no means obvious. If the thoroughly objectionable character of such transactions is recognised, no doubt bankers will be able to do a good deal to discourage it.

THE GOLD STANDARD

The problem of the gold standard in its various aspects, national and international, is a complex and difficult one, and it is one which has given rise to wide differences of opinion among recognised authorities. A detailed discussion of these matters would unduly extend the scope of the present essay.

It may be pointed out, however, that gold has risen considerably in value during the past decade, it is rising rapidly at the present time (1933), and the available evidence supports the belief that it will go on rising in the immediate future.

A currency which is continually rising in value decreases the profits of the trader and the industrialist and acts as an ever-increasing drag on the wheels of industry, and the gold standard as at present worked is obviously open to this very serious objection.

It must further be noted that Great Britain enjoyed a reasonable measure of prosperity before she returned to the gold standard in 1925; her prosperity declined for the whole period during which the gold standard was in operation; and finally abandonment of the gold standard in 1931 has been followed by distinct signs of returning prosperity. The argument is obviously a superficial one, but it cannot be ignored on that account.

Taking due account of all that can be argued for and against, I think it may be fairly said that it is very undesirable that a general return should be made to the gold standard, until means can be devised for counteracting the continual upward tendency in the value of gold, or until a careful examination of the whole problem makes it clear that a better form of currency standard is definitely beyond our reach.

GOVERNMENT CONTROL OF INDUSTRY

It is often argued that private control of industry is a failure and that the only solution of our difficulties is that the control should be placed in the hands of the government. It is interesting to observe therefore that the analysis set forth in the present essay lends no support to this doctrine.

Business men have certainly made mistakes, but politicians have made blunders involving far more serious consequences; for example:—

(i) The policy of European statesmen in rearranging the map of Europe completely ignored economic needs and created many quite unnecessary difficulties which have not yet been overcome.

(ii) The policy of European and American statesmen in regard to war debts and reparations never showed any grasp of the fact that international payments of money are only significant in so far as they lead to changes in the distribution of trade and industry. Agreements were therefore made which could never by any possibility be translated into practice.

(iii) The policy of the United States in regard to tariffs and subsidies was the exact opposite of what was needed in the circumstances actually existing at the time, and contributed largely to the severity of the present crisis.

(iv) Another mistaken policy, and perhaps the most serious blunder of all, was the expansion of credit in the United States during the years immediately preceding the crisis. Technically the Federal Reserve Board was responsible for this particular effort, but there is no doubt that their action was supported by 95 per cent of the citizens of the United States, including of course the politicians, who must therefore accept due share of the blame.

If the control of industry ever passes into the hands of the politicians, it is safe to predict that they will engineer a greater boom followed by a more disastrous slump than any yet known in history.

CHAPTER XX

RECONSTRUCTION

THE ECONOMIST'S DIFFICULTIES

To the ordinary man who has lost his job owing to the crisis, ultimate causes are of somewhat academic importance; what interests him is the question of putting the wheels of industry in motion again so that his employment may be restored. The writer feels therefore that to close his essay without an appreciation of the present situation and a short survey of current problems would be to shirk an important part of his self-appointed task. At the same time it is necessary to warn the reader that the matters referred to in the present chapter are even more controversial than those which have already been discussed.

When an engineer is called upon to design a bridge, let us say, he can in many cases put forward a design which has already been made use of under similar conditions. Even when it is necessary to depart to an appreciable extent from accepted practice he is at least fortified by the knowledge that the properties of his materials are known and that his schemes can be based on methods which have stood the test of experience.

With the economist it is otherwise. The materials with which he is called upon to deal are human needs, human hopes and human fears, and the reactions which are called forth to-day may differ widely from those which might have been expected a generation ago. Again, the whole industrial and commercial structure is undergoing a process of continuous development, and this circumstance may introduce new factors into the problem which were without significance a few years ago.

Unless it is to be entirely featureless a survey of existing problems must be coloured to some extent by personal opinions, and the writer can only plead that the opinions expressed are based upon the arguments which have been set forth in the earlier chapters.

THE LESSONS OF THE PAST

It would no doubt be generally agreed that immediate relief may be too dearly bought if it mortgages the future and leaves mankind exposed to similar or perhaps even greater disaster. If a new economic structure is to be erected on a better and surer foundation it is essential that past mistakes should be understood and avoided, and that hardly won experience should be turned to the best advantage.

Over-production in certain directions has shown that the great potential expansion of production due to modern industrial methods should be exploited in the development of new industries designed to raise the general standard of living rather than to existing industries which cater for a less elastic market.

Trade and industry must be given a chance to adapt themselves to existing conditions, and the erection of tariff barriers or the payment of subsidies tending to divert the flow of trade from established channels must be avoided.

Foreign loans should be made with greater regard to the balance of trade, and in particular the whole system of international short term lending requires revision. The expansion of this type of credit has vastly exceeded all legitimate needs, and the whole system requires to be recast with a view to restricting both the type of security and the total volume of money which are involved in such transactions.

The question of an international currency standard requires careful consideration, and an immediate return to the gold standard of the pre-war type would appear to involve very serious risks.

In broad outline such are the lessons of the past.

GOVERNMENT EXPENDITURE

Balancing the budget is a necessary condition of sound finance, and the operation is one which is much more difficult in times of trade depression. The yield of taxes falls off, and the rate of taxation must be increased or expenditure must be reduced.

Increasing taxation is always unpleasant and it has the further objection that it tends to depress trade still further; it is natural therefore that a period of depression should lead to vehement demands for economy in government expenditure.

On the other hand there is a school of thought which argues that reduction of government expenditure is objectionable because it reduces employment, further reduces the yield of taxes, and generally speaking aggravates an already difficult situation.

It is necessary to consider therefore what is the correct policy for a government to adopt in the face of these conflicting opinions.

The answer which I would venture to give to this question is that both schools of thought are right, up to a point. Government expenditure which is embarked on, not because the work is necessary to the community, but mainly because it will relieve unemployment, is nearly always wasteful, and more especially so if men are not employed at their own trades.

In a modern community a certain amount of capital expenditure is necessary, and some of the work is normally carried out by the government. It is not in the general interest of the community that the work should be abandoned altogether, nor is it desirable that it should be pressed forward in times of prosperity and suspended in times of depression; evidently the correct thing to aim at is to try to adhere to a uniform programme based on sound estimates of real requirements.

As to the possibility that government work might be reduced in times of prosperity and pushed forward in times of depression, it is I think clear that the actual carrying out of such a scheme presents serious practical difficulties. It assumes that the requirements of the community and the incidence of trade depressions can be estimated with greater accuracy than would actually seem to be the case. It also assumes that workers can be diverted from industry whereas in fact the unemployed may not be of the right trades. It further assumes that the employment of money in this way will not react unfavourably on trade and industry, for it must be remembered that an ample supply of funds at low rates of interest is one of the conditions which is necessary for the restoration of trade.

It would appear then that the correct policy for the government to pursue in regard to expenditure is to maintain existing services at their normal level on both ordinary and capital account, subject to the following conditions:—

Firstly, that the balancing of the budget is not interfered with.

Secondly, that expenditure whether on capital account or otherwise is employed on supplying real needs.

Thirdly, that the money required can be made available without prejudice to the requirements of trade and industry.

If these conditions are not complied with government expenditure may retard the return to prosperity instead of promoting it.

ASSISTING RECOVERY

Evidently the first step towards recovery is to remove all known causes of instability and thus lay a secure foundation on which the new economic structure is to rest. There are also certain other points which appear to be worthy of consideration.

The question of government expenditure has already been discussed in the previous section. The rules which should be followed by individuals in the management of their private affairs are based on similar principles. Subject to the proviso that expenditure is not undertaken on such a scale as to limit the supply of cheap credit, it would appear to be desirable that individuals should adopt, so far as possible, their normal methods of living and should spend money on the same scale as they would normally adopt in more prosperous times. By thus anticipating the return of prosperity they will not only help to promote recovery but will also establish conditions which will serve to make recovery, when it does come, less violent and abrupt.

In Chapter IX four factors were referred to as being likely to increase the profits of trade and industry and thereby promote the process of recovery; they were:—

(i) Reductions in wages.
(ii) Reduction of fixed charges by liquidation.
(iii) Reduction of rates of interest.
(iv) Curtailment of production.

The question then arises, Can anything be done to strengthen these influences, and thereby assist the process of recovery? Let us consider therefore how the action of these various factors may be assisted.

The question of reducing wages during a slump has already been referred to. Circumstances vary widely in different countries and reductions of wages may be desirable in certain cases. For the reasons already given, however, reductions in wages do not usually provide the best solution.

Reduction of fixed charges by liquidation is a process which is largely in the hands of the individuals concerned. If bondholders would remember the parable of the unjust steward, and adjust their claims to the debtors' ability to pay, operations of this character would be simplified and everybody would benefit.

The other two factors, the reduction in rates of interest and the curtailment of production, are matters in which both government and private individuals can do much to help. The actual measures to be taken naturally depend upon circumstances.

There remains yet another and very controversial expedient, namely, adjustment of the currency. It cannot be denied that adjustment of the price level through the medium of the currency may sometimes be desirable, and that it is an expedient which can be successfully employed under certain conditions. Under the leadership of Great Britain a number of countries have put through this operation with conspicuous success. But it is equally undeniable that ill-considered measures may lead to disaster, and it is necessary that the operation should be skilfully carried out under favourable conditions. It would be impossible to discuss the matter more fully here.

The process of reconstruction presents itself in somewhat different form to different countries and to different industries. A brief survey of some of these problems may be of interest.

AGRICULTURE

Agriculture is the oldest and most important industry in the world, and it has suffered to an abnormal extent during the present crisis. Its special difficulties may be summed up as follows:—

Firstly, the introduction of machinery has caused a considerable displacement of labour, and has tended to increase output.

Secondly, the demand is inelastic and shows little power of expansion with increasing prosperity.

Thirdly, the replacement of horse transport by motor transport has increased the available output of food supplies.

Fourthly, the opening up of new areas and the more intense cultivation of those already in use have been stimulated by tariffs.

These factors, supplemented by others of a more general character already referred to, have led to over-production.

Fifthly, agriculture is in the hands of innumerable individuals who act independently of one another, and in this respect it compares unfavourably with the majority of industrial occupations. It compares even less favourably with those occupations which are commonly referred to as the "sheltered trades," and which now include a large and increasing proportion of the whole population. As matters stand a drastic fall in agricultural prices is the only means by which production can be reduced.

Countries which import agricultural products naturally protect their own farmers, and the brunt of the trouble has therefore fallen on those countries which are exporters of such commodities. Since reductions are essential, it would be to the advantage of such countries to devise means for bringing about the necessary limitation of production as quickly and as expeditiously as possible. When production has been adequately reduced a rise in prices may be looked for, but not before.

FRANCE

Let us now take a glance at some of the problems which are especially acute in the case of particular countries, and let us begin with France.

The French are thrifty people, and there is always a tendency in France for savings to outrun the available supply of appropriate investments. In the past a large volume of French savings has found its way into foreign investments of one sort or another, but not with very satisfactory results; large sums were invested in Russia before the war, for example, and have been completely lost. The result is that the French investor has become unsympathetic in regard to foreign investments, and rightly so.

This pressure of savings, and the lack of adequate home investment, has compelled the French banks to buy gold, but it is obvious that this expedient provides neither a permanent nor a satisfactory solution to the problem.

The ultimate solution would appear to be that the French nation must learn to spend more and save less, but no mere foreigner is in a position to suggest how this desirable condition of affairs is to be brought about.

Meanwhile French banks will no doubt continue to buy gold, and the world at large will suffer from a shortage of the precious metal, and will experience difficulty in making use of it as a medium of international currency.

GERMANY

During the past decade Germany's whole economic system has been thrown into confusion by foreign interference. On the one hand she has been under political pressure from her former enemies to pay large sums in respect of reparations, and on the other hand she has been beset by international lenders anxious to provide her with the money to pay these reparations and more besides. There is reason to believe that this Gilbertian situation is now at an end.

There still remains of course an enormous volume of commercial debts which will have to be dealt with in due course, but it is unlikely that the creditors will possess the same power of mischievous interference as their political predecessors, and in course of time they too will have to face realities.

Like other nations throughout the world Germany has had to face falling prices and dislocation of trade, and the previous collapse of her currency has made her extremely reluctant to run any further risks in the same direction. She has therefore been compelled to adopt the more difficult expedient of making a direct attack on rates of interest and rates of wages.

Unless the political strain proves too great to be borne, there appears to be reason to hope that Germany is nearing the end of her troubles.

GREAT BRITAIN

In 1930 Great Britain was faced with an unbalanced budget, a very serious amount of unemployment and a balance of trade showing a serious excess of imports over exports, and all these troubles appeared to be increasing rather than diminishing.

The balancing of the budget, never an easy matter in times of crisis, has been successfully accomplished, and has made it possible to reduce the value of money without losing control of the situation.

When the trouble with the trade balance is an excess of imports, the required adjustment is more easily effected than when it is necessary to deal with an excess of exports. The abandonment of the gold standard and the introduction of tariffs were both appropriate remedies and there is reason to hope that they are proving effective.

The abandonment of the gold standard has also checked the fall in prices, and there are indications that trade is beginning to recover.

In 1925 the welfare of industry was sacrificed to what appeared to be the interests of traders and financiers, and it is of vital importance that this mistake should not be repeated. Provided that no false steps are taken in the immediate future and provided also that she is not involved in troubles created by the blunders of others, there seems to be good reason to hope that Great Britain has surmounted the worst of her difficulties.

THE SMALL NATIONS OF EUROPE

The craving for political and economic independence and the extensive encouragement of home industries have certainly been carried beyond reasonable limits, and it is essential to recovery that this tendency should be checked. The tendency has been fostered by the willingness of foreign countries to lend money, and the borrowing of money abroad has had the effect of obscuring the real facts of the situation, and the essentially temporary character of such assistance has been overlooked. Much more real progress would have been made if nations had been compelled to face facts, and work out their own salvation in their own way with the minimum of foreign help.

Foreign lending and foreign investment on the scale which has been adopted during the past decade harm both borrower and lender, and a return to this system, while affording temporary relief, could only serve to intensify the ultimate reaction.

THE UNITED STATES OF AMERICA

It is the boast of its citizens that everything in the United States is always done upon the grandest possible scale, and the present crisis is certainly no exception to the rule. The economic blunders which preceded the crisis, the abruptness and intensity of the crisis itself, and the problems of reconstruction which remain for solution are all true to type.

The problems of reconstruction are naturally interconnected, one with another, but it may I think be said that the economic problems of the United States present three main aspects:—

Firstly, there is the problem of balancing the budget, which is a very desirable preliminary to any attempt to adjust the currency. But the risk of uncontrolled inflation is not the only matter of importance which arises in connection with an unbalanced budget; there is also another consequence, which is of very great significance, and which may easily be overlooked.

The reconstruction of the industrial system which is referred to below will need capital, and this capital can only be provided out of the savings of individuals. If these savings are diverted into government loans which are rendered necessary by an unbalanced budget, then the money will be spent on consumable commodities and will not be available for the purposes of reconstruction.

Secondly, there is the problem of increasing the volume of employment by restoring the profits of industry which have been destroyed by the collapse of prices. In other words prices must be increased by reducing the value of money. At the time of writing this view of the situation has been adopted by the United States government, and the gold standard has been abandoned. As to whether the actual methods adopted will produce the desired results it is too early to express an opinion.

Thirdly, there is the problem of the trade balance. Investors have apparently discovered at long last that there is no profit to be obtained from the policy of giving away goods with one hand while refusing to accept payment with the other. In future imports and exports will have to balance, therefore, much more closely than they have done in the past, and the industrial system will have to be reconstructed on that basis.

It would be mere impertinence on the part of an

outsider to offer suggestions as to how these problems are to be solved, but it is I think legitimate to point out that certain types of solution are economically impossible.

There appears to be an idea for example that the payment of war debts by Europe would simplify the problem of balancing the budget, and this is no doubt correct. It is overlooked, however, that such payments must have an adverse effect on the export trade and must therefore increase the volume of unemployment. Nothing is to be gained therefore by proceeding on these lines.

Again, it has been suggested that a reduction of tariffs would increase international trade, and would thereby benefit employment. There do not appear to be any solid grounds, however, for any such conclusion. An expansion of exports tends to produce a corresponding expansion of imports and the total volume of employment is not seriously altered. Considerations which are important in the case of small countries are without significance in the case of a large country like the United States, which contains within its own borders nearly all the requisites for a complete and self-supporting economic existence.

The fundamental fact is that no material help can be obtained in this matter by means of foreign co-operation of any kind. In this particular case the lack of adjustment in the economic structure is an internal disorder, and the remedy is to be sought within the boundaries of the country itself and not from without.

The greatest danger is that people may come to believe that the whole business can be settled by adjustments of the currency designed to raise the price level. Such adjustments are necessary, but they do not solve the whole problem. Serious alterations in the industrial structure are also essential and will require time for their development, and real prosperity will only return when this problem of reconstruction is taken seriously in hand.

CONCLUSION

The individual citizen probably takes the view that Economics is a subject for experts, and believes that the results are beyond both his understanding and his control, but a careful examination of the position discloses the fact that his responsibilities are not so easily evaded.

Everyone who has more than enough money to support a bare existence must decide whether to spend the balance of his money or save it, and the aggregate result of these decisions determines the total volume of national savings.

Again, the money which is saved may be directly invested or may be deposited in a bank, and the nature of this decision and the form of investment which is ultimately selected are matters of fundamental national and international importance.

It must also be remembered that governments

have to make important decisions which affect both the currency and the trade balance, and the fate of governments depends upon the popular vote. If then the ordinary citizen supports a faulty policy through ignorance of elementary economic principles, he has no one to thank for his misfortunes but himself.

Knowledge is power, and the nations of the world, who are suffering from the consequences of an economic disaster, can obtain control of events only by acquiring a knowledge of the economic forces which control their industrial life, and by applying this knowledge to the settlement of economic problems. Lack of knowledge leaves the world at the mercy of cranks and place-hunters, who deceive themselves as well as their victims, and who mistake self-confidence and verbosity for the real knowledge which can only be acquired by careful and pains-taking study of the facts.

The acquisition of precise and detailed knowledge of economic problems, and the wide dissemination of that knowledge, are the sole means by which mankind may secure control of its own destinies, for there is no other road.

REFERENCES

1. A. Marshall: *Principles of Economics* (1895), p. 1; *see also* p. 75.
2. H. Clay: *Economics* (1918), which gives a general discussion of the principle of the division of labour and its implications.
3. J. M. Keynes: *A Treatise on Money* (1930), Vol. II, chap. 30.
4. F. Henderson: *The Economic Consequences of Power Production*, chap. II.
5. F. Henderson: *loc. cit.*, chaps. III and IV.
6. H. Emerson: *Efficiency* (1911).
7. *U.S.A. Bureau of Labour Statistics* (1930).
8. L. J. Barley: *The Riddle of Rationalisation* (1932).
9. A. Marshall: *loc. cit.*, p. 650.
10. *The Macmillan Committee*, pp. 194–196.
11. Sir J. Stamp: *The Financial Aftermath of War* (1932), chap. II.
12. Sir A. Salter: *Recovery* (1932), p. 42.
13. J. M. Keynes: *loc. cit.*, Vol. II, p. 217.
14. Hartley Withers: *Bankers and Credit* (1924) The passage is quoted with approval by C. Rist in the discussion on the *International Gold Problem, Collected Papers discussed before the Royal Institute of International Affairs*, p. 80, and the opinion is also endorsed by R. G. Hawtrey, p. 209.
15. H. Clay: *The Macmillan Committee, Evidence*, Vol. II, p. 255, § 25.
16. Irving Fisher: *Booms and Depressions*, chap. II.
17. *The Macmillan Committee*, p. 166.
    Sir A. Salter: *loc. cit.*, p. 32.
18. J. M. Keynes: *loc. cit.*, Vol. I, chap. 12.
19. For a discussion of French banking policy which has led to the accumulation of gold in French banks *see* C. Rist: *The International Gold Problem*, p. 193 *et seq.*
20. Sir A. Salter: *loc. cit.*, pp. 102–107.
21. N. Crump: in the *Sunday Times* of December 4, 1932.
22. Sir J. Stamp: *loc. cit.*, p. 146.
23. J. M. Keynes: *loc. cit.*, Vol. II, pp. 170–176.
    Sir J. Stamp: *loc. cit.*, chap. IV.
24. Sir A. Salter: *loc. cit.*, chap. III.
25. J. M. Keynes: *The Economic Consequences of Peace.*
26. Sir A. Salter: *loc. cit.*, pp. 142–148.
27. Sir J. Stamp: *loc. cit.*, p. 117.
28. The value of the pound sterling in 1923 varied between 4·7 and 4·36 against a parity of 4·85 dollars, making the ratio 0·97 to 0·90.
29. The rise in wholesale prices between 1913 and 1923 was 59 per cent, making the money ratio 0·63.
30. J. M. Keynes: *A Treatise on Money*, Vol. II, pp. 182–183.
31. J. M. Keynes: *loc. cit.*, Vol. II, p. 184.
32. F. Benham: *British Monetary Policy*, chap. II.
33. Irving Fisher: *loc. cit.*, pp. 80–81 and 86–91.
34. Sir J. Stamp: *The International Gold Problem*, p. 1.
35. J. M. Keynes: *loc. cit.*, Vol. II, p. 304 *et seq.*
36. Irving Fisher: *loc. cit.*, chap. VII.